CONTENTS

A NOTE ABOUT COPYRIGHT

Dear Customer

What does the little © mean and why does it matter?

Your market-leading BPP books, course materials and e-learning materials do not write and update themselves. People write them: on their own behalf or as employees of an organisation that invests in this activity. Copyright law protects their livelihoods. It does so by creating rights over the use of the content.

Breach of copyright is a form of theft – as well as being a criminal offence in some jurisdictions, it is potentially a serious breach of professional ethics.

With current technology, things might seem a bit hazy but, basically, without the express permission of BPP Learning Media:

- Photocopying our materials is a breach of copyright

- Scanning, ripcasting or conversion of our digital materials into different file formats, uploading them to facebook or e-mailing them to your friends is a breach of copyright

You can, of course, sell your books, in the form in which you have bought them – once you have finished with them. (Is this fair to your fellow students? We update for a reason.)

And what about outside the UK? BPP Learning Media strives to make our materials available at prices students can afford by local printing arrangements, pricing policies and partnerships which are clearly listed on our website. A tiny minority ignore this and indulge in criminal activity by illegally photocopying our material or supporting organisations that do. If they act illegally and unethically in one area, can you really trust them?

AAT

Qualification and Credit Framework (QCF)

LEVEL 2 CERTIFICATE IN ACCOUNTING

WORKBOOK

Computerised Accounting Software

2012 Edition

First edition July 2010
Third edition June 2012

ISBN 9781 4453 9497 8
(Previous ISBN 9780 7517 9773 2)

British Library Cataloguing-in-Publication Data
A catalogue record for this book is available from the British
Library

Published by

BPP Learning Media Ltd
BPP House
Aldine Place
London
W12 8AA

www.bpp.com/learningmedia

Printed in the United Kingdom

BPP LEARNING MEDIA'S AAT MATERIALS

Since July 2010 the AAT's assessments have fallen within the **Qualifications and Credit Framework** and most papers are now assessed by way of an on demand **computer based assessment**. BPP Learning Media has invested heavily to ensure our ground breaking materials are as relevant as possible for this method of assessment. In particular, our **suite of online resources** ensures that you are prepared for online testing by allowing you to practice numerous online tasks that are similar to the tasks you will encounter in the AAT's assessments.

The BPP range of resources comprises:

- **Texts**, covering all the knowledge and understanding needed by students, with numerous illustrations of 'how it works', practical examples and tasks for you to use to consolidate your learning. The majority of tasks within the texts have been written in an interactive style that reflects the style of the online tasks we anticipate the AAT will set. Texts are available in our traditional paper format and, in addition, as ebooks which can be downloaded to your PC or laptop.

- **Question Banks**, including additional learning questions plus the AAT's practice assessment and a number of other full practice assessments. Full answers to all questions and assessments, prepared by BPP Learning Media Ltd, are included. Our question banks are provided free of charge in an online environment containing tasks similar to those you will encounter in the AAT's testing environment. This means you can become familiar with being tested in an online environment prior to completing the real assessment.

- **Passcards**, which are handy pocket-sized revision tools designed to fit in a handbag or briefcase to enable you to revise anywhere at anytime. All major points are covered in the Passcards which have been designed to assist you in consolidating knowledge.

- **Workbooks**, which have been designed to cover the units that are assessed by way of project/case study. The workbooks contain many practical tasks to assist in the learning process and also a sample assessment or project to work through.

- **Lecturers' resources**, providing a further bank of tasks, answers and full practice assessments for classroom use, available separately only to lecturers whose colleges adopt BPP Learning Media material. The practice assessments within the lecturers' resources are available in both paper format and online in e format.

This Workbook for *Computerised Accounting Software* has been written specifically to ensure complete yet concise coverage of the AAT's new learning outcomes and assessment criteria. It is fully up-to-date as at June 2012 and reflects both the AAT's unit guide and the practice assessment provided by the AAT updated to incorporate the 20% standard VAT rate.

The format of the Computerised Accounting assessment is subject to revision and tutors and students should ensure they check the latest AAT guidance for Computerised Accounting before preparing for the assessment.

Each chapter contains:

- Clear, step-by-step explanation of the topic
- Logical progression and linking from one chapter to the next
- Numerous hands-on exercises and illustrations
- Interactive tasks within the chapter itself, with answers following the chapters, before the Practice Assessments
- Test your learning questions, again with answers supplied following the chapters, before the Practice Assessments

The emphasis in all tasks and questions is on the practical application of the skills acquired.

If you have any comments about this book, please e-mail paulsutcliffe@bpp.com or write to Paul Sutcliffe, Senior Publishing Manager, BPP Learning Media Ltd, BPP House, Aldine Place, London W12 8AA.

VAT

You will find examples and questions throughout this Text which need you to calculate or be aware of a rate of VAT. This is stated at 20% in these examples and questions, unless information provided indicates the item is VAT exempt or zero-rated.

A NOTE ON TERMINOLOGY

On 1 January 2012, the AAT moved from UK GAAP to IFRS terminology. Although you may be used to UK terminology, you need to now know the equivalent international terminology for your assessments.

The following information is taken from an article on the AAT's website and describes how the terminology changes impact on students studying for each level of the AAT QCF qualification.

What is the impact of IFRS terms on AAT assessments?

The list shown in the table that follows gives the 'translation' between UK GAAP and IFRS.

UK GAAP	IFRS
Final accounts	Financial statements
Trading and profit and loss account	**Income statement or Statement of comprehensive income**
Turnover or Sales	Revenue or Sales Revenue
Sundry income	Other operating income
Interest payable	Finance costs
Sundry expenses	Other operating costs
Operating profit	Profit from operations
Net profit/loss	Profit/Loss for the year/period
Balance sheet	**Statement of financial position**
Fixed assets	Non-current assets
Net book value	Carrying amount
Tangible assets	Property, plant and equipment
Reducing balance depreciation	Diminishing balance depreciation
Depreciation/Depreciation expense(s)	Depreciation charge(s)
Stocks	Inventories
Trade debtors or Debtors	Trade receivables
Prepayments	Other receivables
Debtors and prepayments	Trade and other receivables
Cash at bank and in hand	Cash and cash equivalents
Trade creditors or Creditors	Trade payables

UK GAAP	IFRS
Accruals	Other payables
Creditors and accruals	Trade and other payables
Long-term liabilities	Non-current liabilities
Capital and reserves	Equity (limited companies)
Profit and loss balance	Retained earnings
Minority interest	Non-controlling interest
Cash flow statement	**Statement of cash flows**

This is certainly not a comprehensive list, which would run to several pages, but it does cover the main terms that you will come across in your studies and assessments. However, you won't need to know all of these in the early stages of your studies – some of the terms will not be used until you reach Level 4. For each level of the AAT qualification, the points to bear in mind are as follows:

Level 2 Certificate in Accounting

The IFRS terms do not impact greatly at this level. Make sure you are familiar with 'receivables' (also referred to as 'trade receivables'), 'payables' (also referred to as 'trade payables'), and 'inventories'. The terms sales ledger and purchases ledger – together with their control accounts – will continue to be used. Sometimes the control accounts might be called 'trade receivables control account' and 'trade payables control account'. The other term to be aware of is 'non-current asset' – this may be used in some assessments.

Level 3 Diploma in Accounting

At this level you need to be familiar with the term 'financial statements'. The financial statements comprise an 'income statement' (profit and loss account), and a 'statement of financial position' (balance sheet). In the income statement the term 'revenue' or 'sales revenue' takes the place of 'sales', and 'profit for the year' replaces 'net profit'. Other terms may be used in the statement of financial position – eg 'non-current assets' and 'carrying amount'. However, specialist limited company terms are not required at this level.

Level 4 Diploma in Accounting

At Level 4 a wider range of IFRS terms is needed, and in the case of Financial statements (FNST), are already in use – particularly those relating to limited companies. Note especially that an income statement becomes a 'statement of comprehensive income'.

Note: The information above was taken from an AAT article from the 'assessment news' area of the AAT website (www.aat.org.uk).

ASSESSMENT STRATEGY

Computerised Accounting Software (CMPA) is assessed at Level 2. The unit may be assessed either using workplace evidence (which is locally assessed by a centre) or by completing the computer-based assessment (which is set centrally and assessed by the AAT).

The assessment is in **two sections**. You must prove competence in each section to be successful.

- **Section 1** asks you to input data into a computerised accounting package and produce documents and reports

- **Section 2** asks you to complete short answer questions

The time allowed to complete this Computerised accounting assessment is 3 hours. Additional time up to a maximum of 1 hour may be scheduled by your tutor to allow for delays due to computer issues, such as printer queues and uploading documents.

The purpose of the assessment is to allow the learner to demonstrate the skills and knowledge necessary to use computerised accounting software at Level 2.

The assessment is designed to allow the use of any accounting software package.

Competency

The assessment material will normally be provided by the AAT, delivered online and assessed locally. Learners will be required to demonstrate competence in all sections of the assessment.

For the purpose of assessment the competency level for AAT assessment is set at 70%. The Level Descriptor that follows describes the ability and skills students at this level must successfully demonstrate to achieve competence.

QCF Level descriptor for Level 2

Summary

Achievement at Level 2 reflects the ability to select and use relevant knowledge, ideas, skills and procedures to complete well-defined tasks and address straightforward problems. It includes taking responsibility for completing tasks and procedures and exercising autonomy and judgement subject to overall direction or guidance.

Knowledge and understanding

- Use understanding of facts, procedures and ideas to complete well-defined tasks and address straightforward problems.

- Interpret relevant information and ideas.

- Be aware of the types of information that are relevant to the area of study or work.

Application and action

- Complete well-defined, generally routine tasks and address straightforward problems.

- Select and use relevant skills and procedures.

- Identify, gather and use relevant information to inform actions.

- Identify how effective actions have been.

Autonomy and accountability

- Take responsibility for completing tasks and procedures.

- Exercise autonomy and judgement subject to overall direction or guidance.

Conduct of the assessment

The following information was taken from the AAT guidance for Computerised accounting on the AAT website at the time of publishing.

The assessment material will be provided by the AAT and delivered online through LearnPlus. Learners will be required to demonstrate competence in both sections of the assessment.

Printing facilities will need to be made available to students undertaking the assessment (or see 'alternatives to print' below).

- Training providers should consider how printing will be managed in the assessment with regards to the resources available.

- Training providers are reminded that candidates should not leave the assessment room with live material, and an invigilator must remain in the room at all times during the assessment.

- Training providers are permitted to allow individual candidates to print out their assessment book if they feel it improves usability when working on the accounting software.

The time allowed to complete the assessment is **3 hours**. Training providers can schedule up to 1 hour of extra time to allow for possible hardware issues such as printer queues. We recommend that training providers take this option.

It is suggested that candidates take a short supervised break after Task 1.6.

The system software date, company details and the date of the financial year will be given in the assessment book. These details should be entered at the start of the assessment; this set-up does not form part of the standards, therefore training providers may assist candidates with this.

The accounting package should contain the software default predetermined nominal ledger codes, a copy of which should be made available to candidates at the start of the assessment.

The candidate is asked to back up work to a suitable storage medium. This can be of the assessor's choosing, although the medium chosen must comply with the terms and conditions of this assessment (eg a non-portable storage medium such as a secure area in a local or networked hard drive). Candidates should be told which back up medium to use at the start of the assessment.

Alternatives to print

The candidate is asked to print documents and reports that will provide information needed for marking purposes. However, if this information is not provided by the specified documents and reports as generated by the computer package you are using, then the training provider may ask the candidate to print an alternative document.

BPP
LEARNING MEDIA

If the training provider's computerised accounting system allows for the generation of PDFs, these can be generated instead of hard copy prints. Screenshots saved as image files are also acceptable.

Submitting the assessment

All printed material should be clearly titled and labelled with the candidate's name and membership number. After the assessment, printed material should be made available to the assessor to be marked alongside the student's assessment book. There is no requirement for printed material to be uploaded to LearnPlus.

If candidates are using print-outs as evidence, the only document the candidate is required to upload at the end of the assessment is their assessment booklet.

If candidates have generated PDFs or screenshots instead of printing, these documents should be uploaded to LearnPlus with their assessment book.

The AAT Code of Practice states that training providers must ensure that all printed assessment material is kept in a safe and secure environment for a period of at least three years. These documents can be scanned and saved digitally, but the material must be available for the AAT or regulators to review if required.

AAT UNIT GUIDE

Computerised Accounting Software (CMPA)

Introduction

Please read this document in conjunction with the standards for all relevant units.

The purpose of the unit

This unit is about using a computerised accounting application to:

- Input and process data for business transactions including sales and purchases, receipts and payments.
- Prepare management and period-end reports.

Learning objectives

A computerised software accounting user at this level can select and use a wide range of accounting software tools and techniques for information that are at times non-routine or unfamiliar.

Learning outcomes

This unit consists of three learning outcomes.

(1) Access, enter and edit accounting information.

(2) Select and use tools and techniques to process business transactions.

(3) Produce accounting documents and summary reports to meet requirements.

Further details are provided in the following table and subsequent paragraphs.

QCF unit	Learning outcome	Assessment criteria	Covered in Chapter
Computerised Accounting Software (CMPA)	Access, enter and edit accounting information	Describe the sources and characteristics of accounting data.	1
		Set up and create new accounting data records accurately to meet requirements.	2 – 3
		Locate and display accounting data records to meet requirements.	2 – 3
			3
		Check data records meet needs using IT tools, making corrections as necessary.	2 – 3
		Respond appropriately to data entry error messages.	1
		Describe the risks to data security and procedures used for data protection.	1
		Apply local and/or legal guidelines for the storage and use of data.	
	Select and use tools and techniques to process business transactions	Select and use appropriate tools and techniques to enter and process transactions.	2 – 3
		Review transaction process and identify any errors.	2 – 3
		Respond appropriately to any transactions errors and problems.	2 – 3
		Select and use appropriate tools and techniques to process period-end routines.	3

QCF unit	Learning outcome	Assessment criteria	Covered in Chapter
	Produce accounting documents and summary reports to meet requirements	Describe what information is required and how to present it.	1
		Prepare and generate accounting documents.	2 – 3
		Prepare and generate management reports as required.	3
		Import and export data and link to other systems and software	3

Delivery guidance

Learners must be able to perform tasks or answer questions on the topics and procedures specified below. They must be able to take and print screen shots of their work. They must be able to refer to the help guidelines included in the software package and make use of these as required.

It is recognised that a variety of accounting software packages are available and can be used but the one chosen must be capable of performing the procedures outlined below.

For assessment purposes the software should be set up with the system software date, company details and the date of the financial year, all of which will be given in the assessment book. These details should be entered at the start of the assessment; this set-up does not form part of the standards, therefore training providers may assist candidates with this.

Topics and procedures that can be tested

1.   Access, enter and edit accounting information

1.1 Describe the sources and characteristics of accounting data

- Understand what source documentation is used to enter data on to the computer.

- Understand why coding is needed within the accounting system and how to allocate codes to customers' and suppliers' accounts.

- Understand the legal requirements for document retention, eg hard copies

1.2 <u>Set up and create new accounting data records accurately to meet requirements</u>

1.3 <u>Locate and display accounting data records to meet requirements</u>

- Set the software system date, ie today's date, as required.

- Set up, use and amend records and ledger accounts for new and existing credit customers and credit suppliers, using data entry instructions or the appropriate software tool (the wizard). This includes entering credit control details, opening balances brought forward and/or nil opening balances.

- Set up and use nominal ledger accounts, using data entry instructions or the appropriate software tool (the wizard). This includes:

    - Selecting appropriate accounts from the default list of accounts provided by the software.

    - Amending the account names used in the default list of accounts provided by the software, for example change 'sales' to 'sales of product A'.

    - Adding new accounts to the default list of accounts provided by the software.

    - Entering opening balances.

    - Checking opening entries using the trial balance.

1.4 <u>Check data records meet needs using IT tools, making corrections as necessary</u>

1.5 <u>Respond appropriately to data entry error messages</u>

There is also some overlap with LO2

2.3 <u>Respond appropriately to any transactions errors and problems.</u>

- Check own work for accuracy at all times and use appropriate software tools to verify data is correct. Make corrections within limits of responsibility, or follow organisational procedures for reporting errors and problems.

- Respond to software generated error messages or follow organisational procedures for reporting errors and problems.

1.6 <u>Describe the risks to data security and procedures used for data protection</u>

1.7 <u>Apply local and/or legal guidelines for the storage and use of data</u>

Understand:

- The risks to data such as loss and/or theft, illegal copying, poor storage, viruses, unauthorised access to confidential information.

- The possible consequences of these risks.

- Ways to reduce these risks such as use of passwords, how to choose a password in accordance with best practice, backup of computerised data, the use of appropriate file names, proper storage of computerised data including backup copies and virus protection.

Be aware of the basic requirements of the Data Protection Act and relevant organisational policy in relation to security and back up procedures

Back up computerised data to a suitable storage media at regular intervals

2 Select and use tools and techniques to process business transactions

2.1 <u>Select and use appropriate tools and techniques to enter and process transactions</u>

2.2 <u>Review transaction process and identify any errors</u>

2.3 <u>Respond appropriately to any transactions errors and problems</u>

2.4 <u>Select and use appropriate tools and techniques to process period-end routines</u>

There is also some overlap with LO1

1.3 <u>Locate and display accounting data records to meet requirements</u>

1.4 <u>Check data records meet needs using IT tools, making corrections as necessary</u>

- Process transactions involving different rates of VAT:
  - Standard rate
  - Zero rate
  - Not applicable

  The rate of VAT will always be given

- Post entries to record sales and purchases invoices and credit notes, in batches or singly, using if necessary, nominal ledger accounts not previously set up.

- Post payments received from credit customers and payments made to credit suppliers. Payments in this instance can comprise cash, cheques, and automated payments. Match payments to given balances, invoices and credit notes or post as a payment on account. Set off payments (contra entries) and settlement discounts will NOT be tested.

- **Post entries to record:**
  - Cash purchases and sales – payment made/received by cash, cheque or debit card but NOT credit card
  - Sundry income received by cash or cheque

- Payments for items other than the purchase of goods, made by cash, cheque, debit card or automated payment, but NOT credit card

- Petty cash transactions including re-imbursement of petty cash float

- Standing orders and direct debits as a single transaction only

- Transfers between bank accounts

- Irrecoverable debts written off

- Bank interest paid and received

■ Post journal entries, or use an appropriate tool in the software package where relevant, to:

- Amend opening balances

- Remove duplicate entries

- Correct given and own errors

■ Process period-end routines:

- Extract a trial balance. Trace and correct own errors

- Update the bank account where necessary from a bank statement and prepare a bank reconciliation statement. If the bank reconciliation statement does not agree trace and correct own errors. The opening balance on the bank statement will always be equal to the opening bank balance.

- Clear month end turnover totals

3 Produce accounting documents and summary reports to meet requirements

3.1 Describe what information is required and how to present it

3.2 Prepare and generate accounting documents

3.3 Prepare and generate management reports as required

There is also some overlap with LO1

1.3 Locate and display accounting data records to meet requirements

■ Understand who requires accounting data and in what form it is required.

■ Data includes details of customers and suppliers, ledger balances, bank reconciliation statement, audit trail, aged trade receivables/trade payables analysis, statements of account, monthly sales figures.

■ Understand the importance of generating the appropriate accounting documents and management reports for the end user

Prepare and print:

- Customers and suppliers lists.
- Sales, purchases and returns day books.
- All sales ledger (customer) accounts, or specific sales ledger (customer) accounts only.
- All purchases ledger (supplier) accounts, or specific purchases ledger (supplier) accounts only.
- All nominal ledger accounts, or specific nominal ledger accounts only.
- Petty cash and all bank accounts, or specific accounts only.
- The journal.
- A trial balance.
- Bank reconciliation statement.
- Audit trail.
- Aged trade receivables/trade payables analysis.
- Statements of account to be sent to credit customers.
- Letters to customers regarding overdue accounts.

For assessment purposes note there are alternatives to 'print' specified

3.4 <u>Import and export data and link to other systems and software</u>

- Process simple data export tasks to other systems and software such as:
    - Export a customer statement for e-mail
    - Export aged trade receivables/trade payables analysis to a spreadsheet
    - Screen shots
- Be aware of and able to answer questions on:
    - All types of data that can be exported to other systems and software
    - Types of data that can be imported from other systems and software and in what format

Learners will NOT be required to:

- Generate income statement accounts and statement of financial position.
- Post depreciation or other receivables and other payables.
- Prepare or update budgets.
- Prepare invoices or credit notes.
- Create or use product/inventory records.
- Set up recurring entries for standing orders and direct debits

SAGE SOFTWARE

Do students have to use Sage to complete this unit?

No. Students **do not** have to use Sage in their AAT Computerised Accounting Software assessment.

The AAT recognise that a variety of accounting software packages are available and can be used. The only stipulation the AAT make is that the package used must be capable of performing the procedures outlined in the learning outcomes and assessment criteria.

Do students need access to Sage software to use this Workbook?

Students that don't have Sage software may still pick up some useful information from this book, for example from Chapter 1 and the practice assessments.

However, those students with access to Sage will find it easier to work through the practical exercises than users of other accounting software packages.

Refer to the next page for details of how Sage software may be bought, for educational purposes, at very reasonable prices.

Why does this Workbook refer to Sage Instant?

To explain and demonstrate the skills required in this unit, it is necessary to provide practical examples and exercises. This requires the use of computerised accounting software.

This Workbook provides examples taken from Sage Instant Accounts.

What version do I need?

The illustrations in this Workbook are taken from Sage Instant Accounts 2012.

Sage upgrade their software regularly. However, many features and functions remain the same from version to version. For this reason, it is expected that this Workbook will remain valid for a number of future versions of Sage.

Some training centres may use different Sage packages or different versions of Sage. Although the screens and menus may appear slightly different you should still be able to perform the tasks contained in this workbook.

How do I buy Sage software?

Colleges

If this book is used by students in a college environment, the college will need Sage installed on student computers. This publication is based on Sage Instant Accounts 2012 (version 18) but colleges may use a different version of Sage or a different Sage product such as Sage Accounts 50. Sage Instant and Sage 50 packages are very similar in their operation with Sage 50 Accounts being aimed at larger businesses.

Colleges wanting to purchase Sage products should **contact Sage** in the UK on 0800 44 77 77, or email store@sage.com

Individual students

Individual students are able to buy **Sage Instant Accounts** from BPP Learning Media for a very reasonable price. This must be for educational purposes. For details you should contact BPP Learning Media customer services on 0845 075 1100 or email learningmedia@bpp.com

Are Sage data files provided with this book?

No. Sage data files aren't provided because the material is written in such a way that they aren't required.

New installations of Sage allow users to access a blank ledger suitable for experimenting. Instructions are provided in this book that enable a new blank ledger to be created.

chapter 1:

ACCOUNTING DATA AND DATA SECURITY

---

chapter coverage 📖

This chapter is concerned with the sources and characteristics of accounting data, and data security. Your organisation's data needs to be kept secure because it is valuable for business reasons and also because in some situations it is against the law to lose it, misuse it, or let it fall into the wrong hands.

The topics covered in this chapter are:

- ✍ Accounting data
- ✍ Risks to data
- ✍ Passwords
- ✍ The Data Protection Act 1998
- ✍ Copyright
- ✍ Document retention
- ✍ Healthy, safe, secure and well-organised computing

ACCOUNTING DATA

Accounting data captured and stored in an organisation's computerised accounting system comes from a variety of **internal** and **external** sources.

Internal information

This is data collected from **within the organisation**, of which the following are examples.

Accounting records

A system for collecting transactions data, for example, sales and purchases, is essential. Accounts receivable ledgers, accounts payable ledgers, general ledgers, cash books and other accounting records all hold information that may be of great value.

To maintain accuracy and security of accounting records, an organisation operates **controls** over transactions, which also give rise to valuable information. An inventory control system, for example, will include details of purchase orders, goods received notes, goods returned notes and so on, which can be analysed to **provide management information** about speed of delivery, say, or the quality of supplies.

Staff records

Information about **staff** will be held, possibly linked to the **payroll** system. Additional information may be obtained from this source if, say, a project is being costed and it is necessary to ascertain the availability and rate of pay of different levels of staff, or the need for and cost of recruiting staff from outside the organisation.

Production data

Depending upon what the organisation produces, production data could include machine capacity, fuel consumption, movement of people, materials, work in progress, set up times and so on.

Timesheets

Many **service** businesses, for example, accountants and solicitors, need to keep detailed records of the **time spent** on various activities, both to justify fees to clients and to assess the efficiency of operations.

External data and information

An organisation's files (paper and computerised) include external information such as invoices, letters, e-mails, advertisements and so on **received from customers** and **suppliers**.

Sometimes **additional external information** is needed, requiring an active search outside the organisation. The following sources may be identified:

(a) The government

(b) Advice or information bureaux

(c) Consultancies

(d) Newspaper and magazine publishers

(e) There may be specific reference works which are used in a particular line of work

(f) Libraries and information services

(g) Increasingly, businesses link directly to each other's systems, for example via Electronic Data Interchange (EDI)

Electronic sources of information have become dominant in recent years. Many information provision services are now provided via the **internet**.

As the rate of internet use increases, greater numbers of people and organisations are using it to source information on a vast range of topics. The **websites** of many of the sources identified above would include general information that may be useful.

Many reputable businesses now have Facebook and Twitter pages, which provide another possible source of information.

Whether using traditional or web-based sources, it is important to ensure the organisation or person providing the information is **credible**.

Characteristics of data and information

Good information has a number of specific qualities: the mnemonic **ACCURATE** is a useful way of remembering them.

Quality	Example
Accurate	Figures should **add up**, if **rounding** is used it should be appropriate, there should be **no typos**, items should be allocated to the **correct category**.
Complete	Information should include everything that it **needs** to include, for example, external data if relevant, or comparative information.
Cost-beneficial	It should not **cost more** to obtain the information than the **benefit** derived from having it. Providers of information should be given efficient means of collecting and analysing it. Presentation should be such that users do not waste time working out what it means.
User-targeted	The **needs of the user** should be borne in mind, for instance senior managers may require summaries.
Relevant	Information that is **not needed** for a decision should be omitted, to avoid information overload. If producing a report, very detailed information should be kept separate from the main part, for example in an **Appendix** at the back of the report.
Authoritative	The **source** of the information should be reliable. This is an increasingly important concern given the huge number of **information sources** available online.
Timely	The information should be available **when it is needed**.
Easy to use	Information should be **clearly presented, not excessively long**, and sent using the **right medium** and **communication channel** (e-mail, telephone, hard-copy report etc). Long reports should have a summary of the main points (an 'Executive summary') at the start of the report.

RISKS TO DATA

Information held on computers needs to be protected from accidental or malicious damage, from interference and from prying eyes. Interference may be just casual – someone playing around with your machine when you're not there – but it can still result in damage, disruption or loss of files.

It is especially important to keep accounting data secure, because:

- It is needed to run the business properly
- It is commercially sensitive and in some cases (eg payroll data, customer's personal data) it may be highly confidential
- It can contain information that might allow access to bank accounts and hence lead to fraud

- Improper access could allow the unauthorised despatch of goods, the issue of credit notes, the writing-off of debts and other accounting and fraudulent transactions.

Physical risks

The computer hardware itself may be stolen or damaged and so may storage media such as CDs, DVDs, USB 'pen drives' and other removable storage media. Dangers include fire, liquid, poorly arranged desks and offices and unauthorised intruders.

The following specific points are relevant to the security of computers and data.

- You may find that your work computer is security tagged in some way. This doesn't prevent it from being stolen, but it may deter a thief because it increases the risk of the computer – and the thief – subsequently being traced.

- Some organisations go as far as to bolt or chain computer equipment to the working surface. However, this still may not prevent determined burglars from opening up the computer boxes and removing the most valuable components, such as the central processing chip, the memory chips, the hard disk and so on.

- Floppy disks (now rare) are magnetic media – strong magnetic fields can destroy or distort the data stored on them. They are also vulnerable to physical damage by bits of dust or grit, heat or liquid. Floppy disks have largely become obsolete because of the availability of optical disks.

- Optical disks (CDs and DVDs) are more difficult to damage than floppy disks, but are sensitive to heat, finger marks and scratching.

Task 1

People are sometimes careless with their computers. Suggest a few simple rules that you could apply at work to protect computer hardware from damage.

(*Answers to Chapter Tasks are provided following the end of Chapter 3*)

Precautions against viruses

A virus is a piece of software that infects programs and data and copies or replicates itself to other computers. Viruses need an opportunity to spread. The programmers of viruses therefore place them where they are most likely to be copied and circulated. The most common method is an e-mail message, but some free files or software (programs such as amusing screensavers that you may be tempted to download from the internet, for instance) may also be infected.

A virus can be activated very easily – often simply by opening an infected e-mail message – and it may have a number of unpleasant effects. It may be:

- Send itself on – without your knowledge – to everyone in your e-mail address book

- Slow down the operation of your computer so much that it becomes virtually unusable

- Delete particular files

- Wipe or reformat the entire hard disk

- Install and start up a program that could do any number of things – display a message, dial a premium phone number (at your expense), alter your files in some way, disable a particular program, send your data to someone who may misuse it, and so on

If a virus enters a large networked system the damage can be enormous. Files, data and system software can all be attacked. Most organisations therefore respond in several ways.

- By operating firewalls (covered later)

- By banning staff from introducing any disks that haven't been virus-checked by the IT department, or by preventing use of disk drives for floppies and CDs altogether

- Above all, by using anti-virus software, which is always on and which watches out for and destroys suspicious items, or at least stops them before they do any damage

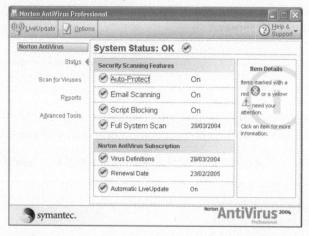

You can help protect yourself simply by being careful. Never install software unless you are absolutely sure it is safe to do so. Never open an e-mail with an attachment unless you trust the person who sent it and are absolutely sure that the attachment is safe.

Most organisations that provide e-mail services – Internet Services Providers (ISPs) – now encourage you to log on to your mail account direct on the internet, so that you can see and check messages before downloading to your computer.

The ISPs often provide software that scans messages and attachments for viruses, as shown in the following illustrations.

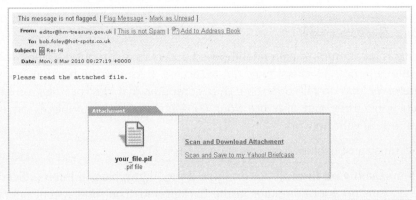

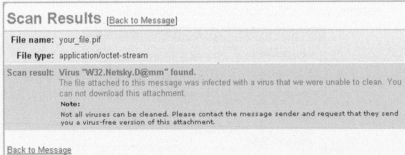

Unfortunately, there are always people creating new, more sophisticated viruses, creating a race between attackers and defenders. All computer users should check for updates to their anti-virus software frequently – at least once a week – and run a system scan equally often.

You should also be aware of hoaxes. These are not viruses at all, but false warnings stating that a document or program contains a virus. Hoaxes are sent in the form of unsolicited e-mail ('spam'), and they encourage people to forward the message to anybody else they can think of that might be affected.

Hoaxes do not do any harm in themselves, although they sometimes request personal information that if disclosed can cause losses and harm.

A hoax in which the sender attempts to acquire sensitive information such as usernames and passwords by pretending to be a trustworthy organisation, is known as phishing.

Other types of hoax are circulated simply because their creators think it is amusing or desirable to create panic and waste the time of individuals and organisations.

Hoaxes are likely to be spotted by spam controls, either on your own computer or at your ISP. If you receive a virus warning, or any message that warns of a problem and requests personal information, it pays to check whether it's a hoax or spoof before acting on it or sending it on to colleagues and friends. Sites such as www.millersmiles.co.uk and www.sturnidae.com/hoax.php are helpful.

Hacking and firewalls

Hacking is an attempt to gain unauthorised access to a computer system, usually over the internet. Hackers may try to access personal information on your computer or may install codes on your computer that destroys files or causes malfunctions. They can also use your computer to cause problems on other computers on your network.

Protection against hackers is provided by a 'Firewall'.

- A **software firewall** (for example Zone Alarm, Norton Internet Security) runs on your computer in the background. The most recent operating systems, such as Windows 7, have a built-in firewall.

- A **hardware firewall** is generally a small box which sits between your computer and your modem. A business network is more likely to have a hardware firewall.

- It is, of course, possible to use both types.

Firewalls have always been important but they have become much more so as more and more people have broadband connections to the internet that are 'always on' (to a hacker, 'always on' means 'always vulnerable').

The main problem with firewalls is that it can take time to get them configured exactly as you want them. Until you have done this, they may attempt to prevent you from doing things that you need to do, such as collecting your e-mail or sharing files with other computers on the network.

Task 2

What option would you choose if the following alert suddenly appeared on your computer screen?

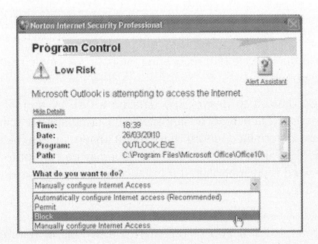

Data recovery

When data items are 'lost' – for instance if you delete a file accidentally – don't panic! Your files can sometimes be recovered even when they seem to have disappeared completely.

This is possible because of the way a computer's filing system works.

When you save a file, the operating system first looks for space on the disk. A large file may be broken up into several smaller chunks to fit various gaps on the disk. The system then identifies the electronic 'addresses' of each storage location, and tags them so that the file can be listed in the file directory.

When you delete a file, the system does NOT delete the actual data, only the address. The data remains, but is now invisible to the file manager system. Later on some data may be stored on top of the original data, but until this happens, the original material can often be recovered.

Your first action should be to check the contents of the *Recycle Bin* (or 'Trash' on an Apple Mac – the icon illustrated above).

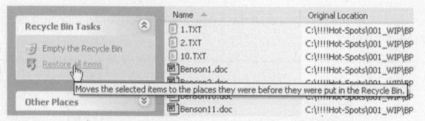

If the files are in the Recycle Bin, recovering the data is a simple matter of clicking on the *Restore* option.

It is surprisingly difficult to destroy the data on a disk by normal (non-violent) means. Experts can often recover items of data using special utility programs, even after very determined efforts have been made to eliminate them. The process can be slow and expensive, and the data may be corrupt to some extent, but when the need is great enough (for instance in a criminal case such as fraud), it may be possible.

The persistence of computer data can therefore present a security problem of its own. Only physical destruction or repeated over-writing or reformatting of the whole disk can remove all traces of data files. Organisations that are very security sensitive may prefer to destroy rather than resell obsolete computers, for this very reason.

Back-ups

Because data and the computers or storage devices on which the information is stored can easily be lost or destroyed, it is vital to take regular copies or back-ups of data. Back-ups are simply copies of the data files. If the data is lost, the back-up copy can be used to reconstitute the data up to the time the back-up was taken. If data changes frequently, back-ups should be taken frequently. The back-ups should be stored away from the original data, in case there is a fire or other disaster at the organisation's premises. Some organisations store back-up files online.

It is normal to keep a series of back-ups (often called generations) in case errors within data have been present for a period of time and have been included in the latest back-ups. Keeping several historical backups can then let the organisation regress further until it finds a good copy.

PASSWORDS

The purpose of a password is to prevent users from accessing data they are not authorised to retrieve.

Task 3

Think about the data and information held on your own computer and how you keep this safe. One suggestion that may help is to attach a password to your screen saver. Then, the original screen can only be restored by keying-in the password.

Besides passwords, what other options can you think of to keep people away from confidential data?

An ideal password is at least eight characters long and consists of a random combination of letters (both capitals and small letters) and numbers, for example *pkTd8z3A*. Although, technically, a good password, the disadvantage is that this would be very difficult to remember.

Assuming you use a password such as this it is important to ensure that the Caps Lock key is not on when you are typing your password, otherwise you will get the small and large letters the wrong way round and your password will be rejected.

Problems with passwords

Passwords are useful as a protection against snoopers and against accidental alterations, though they may not prevent a file from being deleted.

Basic password systems that some popular programs use can easily be by-passed. For example, software is available on the internet that enables you to 'crack' the passwords used by older versions of Microsoft Office programs.

Other possible problems with passwords include the following.

- Many people use a password that is fairly obvious, such as their nickname, or the name of a partner or child, or something that can easily be found out about them, such as their date of birth.

- Others choose a less obvious password (eg pkTd8z3A) and then forget it altogether.

- Many people write down their password where others can easily find it. Putting it on a Post-it note and sticking it to the computer itself is common!

- People may simply tell others what their password is.

Password policy

Organisations can set down a password policy, instructing people not to reveal their passwords to others but this is difficult to enforce. It is difficult to avoid these problems altogether, but some measures can be taken. The organisation can

- Set up the system so that passwords must be a certain length, may not be a real word, and must contain a mixture of letters and numbers.
- Impose passwords on people and not allow individuals to change them.
- Insist that passwords are changed at regular intervals – say every three months. The system itself may require this.

There can be a problem, however, if passwords are a complex combination of upper and lower case letters and numbers and these are changed regularly. They are difficult to remember and this increases the chance that they are written down. A useful approach is to use an easily remembered sentence then use the first letters or some other pattern. For example: 'The rain in Spain falls mainly on the plains', could yield the password TrIsFmOtP.

Changing passwords

If it is suspected that any password has been discovered by, or revealed to, an unauthorised person it should be changed immediately.

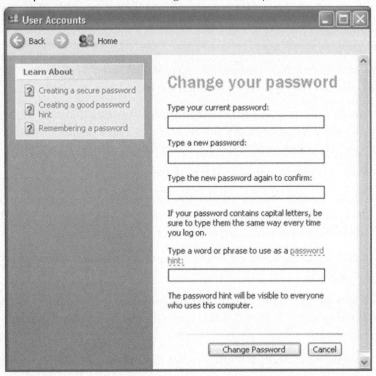

Note that you will be asked to enter your current password before you can change it. This is to prevent others changing your password without your knowledge.

Remembering your password

To help you remember a password, some systems allow you to set a password hint. Inevitably, this is less secure because if the hint reminds you it may well help someone else to work out your password. 'Son's name age' is not a good password hint if your password is 'David11' and you happen to have an eleven-year old son called David! Either make sure that neither your passwords nor your hints are obvious or don't use hints at all.

If you forget a system or program password your only option may be to ask someone with a higher level of access to the system or program to reset it for you. This would mean a new password would be allocated to you so that you can access the system – and you will then be able to change your password yourself to something you can remember.

Be warned though, with some programs it is impossible to unlock a file if you do not know the password. For example, if you encrypt an Excel spreadsheet using a password, you will not be able to access the file. Microsoft has a policy of not giving assistance in these cases (as establishing genuine cases from attempts to bypass security would take far too long).

Encryption

Encryption involves the 'mixing-up' of data so that it becomes unreadable and unusable. It uses a system of keys (rather like passwords) which are used as the basis for encrypting and decrypting the data. You put the key in when encrypting the data and need to put it in again to decrypt it.

Encryption is a standard procedure to use when data is being transmitted over communication lines as you have to be careful about the data being intercepted. If you ever use online banking, your internet link to the bank will use encryption technology. You don't want passwords and account details to be read by others. If you look at the website address and see 'https' at the start, the 's' means that the link has been secured by encryption.

THE DATA PROTECTION ACT 1998

As individuals we are entitled to a certain level of privacy. This places restrictions on organisations in how they use and distribute data and information about people.

In the UK, the legislation covering privacy as it relates to the use of data is the Data Protection Act 1998.

Task 4

Why do you think people might object to organisations distributing data and information about them?

The Act is concerned with 'personal data', which is information about living, identifiable individuals. This can be as little as a name and address: it need not be particularly sensitive information. If it IS sensitive (explained later) then extra care is needed.

The Act gives individuals (data subjects) certain rights and it requires those who record and use personal information (data controllers) to be open about their use of that information and to follow 'sound and proper practices'.

This means that organisation must follow the eight Data Protection Principles as listed and explained below.

If an organisation holds personal information about living individuals on computer or has such information processed on computer by others (for example, its accountants or auditors) the organisation probably needs to 'notify' under the Data Protection Act 1998.

'Notify' means that the organisation has to complete a form about the data it holds and how it is used and send it, with an annual registration fee, to the office of the Information Commissioner.

Organisations have obligations if they receive a written request from an individual asking to see what data it holds about them, or to obtain a copy of it, or to be given an explanation of what it is used for, or who it is given to. The organisation must deal with the request promptly, and in any case within 40 days. The organisation is entitled, if it wishes, to ask for a fee of not more than £10 in which case the 40 days does not begin until this is received.

The eight Data Protection Principles. *Data must be...*

1. **Fairly and lawfully processed**

2. **Processed for limited purposes**

   These two principles mean that when an organisation collects information from individuals it should be honest and open about why it wants the information and it should have a legitimate reason for processing the data.

3. **Adequate, relevant and not excessive**

   Organisations should hold neither too much nor too little data about the individuals in their list. For instance, many companies collect date of birth or age range information from their customers, but in many cases all they actually need to know is that they are over eighteen.

4. **Accurate**

   Personal data should be accurate and up-to-date as far as possible. However, if an individual provides inaccurate information (for example lies about their age) the organisation would not normally be held to account for this.

5. **Not kept longer than necessary**

   There are only exceptional circumstances where personal data should be kept indefinitely. Data should be removed when it is no longer required for audit purposes or when a customer ceases to do business with the data controller.

6. **Processed in accordance with an individual's rights**

   Individuals have various rights including the right to:

   - Be informed of all the information held about them by an organisation

   - Prevent the processing of their data for the purposes of direct marketing

   - Compensation if they can show that they have been caused damage by any contravention of the Act

   - Have any inaccurate data about them removed or corrected.

7. **Secure**

   Organisations should make sure that they provide adequate security for the data, taking into account the nature of the data, and the possible harm to the individual that could arise if the data is disclosed or lost. This should include measures to:

   - Ensure that access to computer records by staff is authorised (for instance a system of passwords).

- Control access to records by people other than staff. For instance care should be taken to ensure screens that may display personal data are not visible to visitors. Also, there should be procedures to verify the identity of callers (including telephone callers) seeking information about an individual.

- Prevent the accidental loss or theft of personal data, for example back-ups and fire precautions.

8. **Not transferred to countries that do not have adequate data protection laws**

If a UK organisation wishes to transfer personal data to a country outside the European Economic Area (EEA) it will either need to ensure there is adequate protection (eg data protection legislation) for the data in the receiving country, or obtain the consent of the individual.

The Data Protection Act 1998 also covers some records held in paper form. These do not need to be notified to the Commissioner, but they should also be handled in accordance with the data protection principles. A set of index cards for a HR system is a typical example of paper records that fall under the Data Protection Act.

Sensitive data

The Act defines eight categories of sensitive personal data, as listed below. If an organisation wishes to hold personal data falling into these categories it is likely that it will need the explicit consent of the individual concerned. It will also need to ensure that its security is adequate for the protection of sensitive data.

- The racial or ethnic origin of data subjects
- Their political opinions
- Their religious beliefs or other beliefs of a similar nature
- Whether they are a member of a trade union
- Their physical or mental health or condition
- Their sexual life
- The commission or alleged commission by them of any offence
- Any details of court proceedings or sentences against them

Task 5

Consider whether your own work involves processing data about individuals and, if so, find out about your own organisation's data protection policies and guidelines.

COPYRIGHT

Copyright law is highly specialised – we only consider matters here relevant to your AAT qualification and to your day-to-day office work.

Copyright is a way of ensuring that the creators of a work have an exclusive right to use it, which means they have the right to stop others from using the work without their permission.

Copyright can be owned by an individual, a group, or an organisation.

There is no need for an author to register copyright with anybody. Usually publishers will mark the work with the international copyright symbol ©, but no notice is necessary. Copyright applies as soon as the material is 'recorded' (in writing, on a cassette tape, in a computer file etc) as opposed to just being in the creator's brain.

The Copyright, Designs and Patents Act 1988

The main legislation (in the UK) is The Copyright, Designs and Patents Act 1988 (CDPA 1988), which covers the following types of 'work'.

- Published materials of all kinds, including text in newspapers, books, magazines, marketing brochures and websites

- Musical works

- Images, paintings, drawings, photographs, and so on

- Sound recordings, films, broadcasts

- Computer programs (for instance any software you use at work)

Most other countries have similar legislation, so don't think you can avoid copyright issues if you copy material from, say, a Canadian website.

Copyright generally applies for a period of 70 years from the end of the calendar year in which the author dies (The Duration of Copyright and Rights in Performances Regulations 1995).

Does it affect you?

Copyright covers the 'form or expression' of an idea, not the idea itself. It covers the way the words or notes or visual images are arranged, not what they convey.

In other words, if you pick up some new ideas about doing your job from this book you can't be prevented from discussing those ideas with your colleagues in a meeting. However, if you copy paragraphs from this book and try to publish them in YOUR OWN book, without the permission of the publishers or author of this book, you are infringing copyright and can be sued for damages.

For the purpose of gathering information at work or for your portfolio you should be aware that under CDPA 1988 copying includes STORING the copyright work in any medium by electronic means. Fortunately, many websites include their own notification that gives you permission to download pages and store them on your computer for, perhaps, 30 days, and perhaps to print out a single copy.

Task 6

Visit the BBC's website and read the Terms and Conditions in full. Get into the habit of doing this for any website that you obtain information from regularly.

Popular fallacies

There are certain provisions in CDPA 1988 relating to the use of short passages, the use of material for educational purposes and its use for private research. But, contrary to popular belief, there are NO exceptions that you can safely rely on when you are 'borrowing' material.

- Do NOT assume you can copy material if you just use a sentence or two.
- Do NOT assume you can copy material if you are only using it for educational purposes.

If there is a dispute the courts will consider the author's rights and the issue of fairness, and this will be different in every case. It is certainly not up to the person copying the material to say what is fair and what is not.

Photocopying

It is normally permissible to photocopy a few pages of someone else's work for research (either commercial or non-commercial) or private study, but again this is subject to the notion of 'fair dealing'.

It is not considered fair, for example, to make a single copy of a whole book (even if it is only a short one), or to make lots of copies of extracts from a book to circulate to every member of your department, say, or to a class of students.

The use of photocopying for educational purposes is limited to 1% of a work in every three months, unless a licensing agreement has been entered into with the publisher and author.

Letters and other written works

If you write a private letter, you own the copyright. The recipient is not entitled to publish it without your permission (unless you write to somebody that normally publishes readers' letters, such as a newspaper). This also applies to your e-mails or postings on an internet notice board.

If, in the course of your job, you write something (a letter, a report, a training programme and so on) you have created it for your employer, and your employer almost certainly owns the copyright.

The same normally applies to any other 'work' you create as part of your job (for instance a word processor macro), unless you have an agreement to the contrary.

File and software sharing

With more and more data and information now stored electronically, in digital files, it has become easier to reproduce and distribute data, for example documents, audio files, software and multi-media files.

In response to widespread unlawful file sharing, for example music files and unlicensed software, copyright owners are beginning to take action against those who infringe their rights. This area of law is still developing.

DOCUMENT RETENTION

There are legal obligations to keep certain documents for certain lengths of time. The Limitations Act 1980 (or the 'Statute of Limitations') deals with documents in general and many business records are covered by specific legislation such as company law, tax law, contract law, charity law, consumer law, employment law, pensions law, health and safety law, and so on.

The table below shows recommended retention periods for various types of documents, but if in doubt you should always seek advice from your manager.

Task 7

Do you think that e-mails sent by or received by businesses need to be kept? Explain your answer.

DOCUMENT	RETAIN FOR...
Accounting and banking records	
Ledger, invoices etc	Six years
Cheques and bills of exchange	Six years
Paying-in counterfoils	Six years
Bank statements	Six years
Instructions to banks (eg standing orders)	Six years
Employee records	
Staff personnel records	Six years after employment ends
Personnel records of senior executives	Permanently
Job applications (rejected candidates)	Up to one year
Time cards and piecework records	Six years
Payroll records	Six years
Expense claims	Six years
Medical records	Permanently
Accident book	Permanently
Insurance	
Correspondence about claims	Three years after claim is settled
Insurance schedules	Seven years
Public liability, product liability and employers' liability policies	Permanently
Contractual and trust agreements	
Simple contracts, eg with customers or suppliers	Six years after contract expires
Contracts under seal (eg related to land and buildings)	12 years after contract expires
Trust deeds (eg a mortgage)	Permanently
Statutory returns, records and registers, board meetings	
All statutory registers	Permanently
Notices, circulars and board minutes	Permanently

HEALTHY, SAFE, SECURE AND WELL-ORGANISED COMPUTING

Possibly the biggest threat to the security of the data that you are responsible for at work is … YOU! If you are not taking enough care – because you are tired, or unwell, or your mind is elsewhere, or you are just having a bad day – there is a very good chance that you will make mistakes, accidentally delete or overwrite a file, spill coffee and so on.

Getting set for work

The Display Screen Equipment regulations offer good advice about efficient, healthy, safe and secure computer work and the main points are summarised below.

Getting comfortable

- Adjust your chair and Visual Display Unit (VDU) to find the most comfortable position for your work. As a guide, your forearms should be approximately horizontal and your eyes the same height as the top of the VDU.

- Make sure you have enough work space to take whatever documents or other equipment you need.

- Try different arrangements of keyboard, screen, mouse and documents to find the best arrangement for you. A document holder may help you avoid awkward neck and eye movements.

- Arrange your desk and VDU to avoid glare, or bright reflections on the screen. This will be easiest if neither you nor the screen is directly facing windows or bright lights. Adjust curtains or blinds to prevent unwanted light.

- Make sure there is space under your desk to move your legs freely. Move any obstacles such as boxes or equipment.

- Avoid excess pressure from the edge of your seat on the backs of your legs and knees. A footrest may be helpful.

The keyboard and mouse

- Adjust your keyboard to get a good keying position. A space in front of the keyboard is helpful for resting the hands and wrists when not keying.

- Try to keep your wrists straight when keying. Keep a soft touch on the keys and do not overstretch your fingers. Good keyboard technique is important.

- Position the mouse within easy reach, so it can be used with the wrist straight. Sit upright and close to the desk, so you do not have to work with your mouse arm stretched. Move the keyboard out of the way if it is not being used.

- Support your forearm on the desk, and do not grip the mouse too tightly.

- Rest your fingers lightly on the buttons and do not press them overly hard.

Reading the screen

- Adjust the brightness and contrast controls on the screen to suit lighting conditions in the room.

- Make sure the screen surface is clean.

- In setting up software, choose options giving text that is large enough to read easily on your screen. Select colours that are easy on the eye (avoid red text on a blue background, or *vice versa*).

- Individual characters on the screen should be sharply focused and should not flicker or move. If they do, the VDU may need servicing or adjustment.

Posture and breaks

- Do not sit in the same position for long periods. Make sure you change your posture as often as practicable. Some movement is desirable, but avoid repeated stretching to reach things you need (if this happens a lot, rearrange your workstation).

- Most jobs provide opportunities to take a break from the screen, eg to do filing or photocopying. Make use of them.

- If there are no such natural breaks in your job, your employer should plan for you to have rest breaks.

- Frequent short breaks are better than fewer long ones.

CHAPTER OVERVIEW

- Both equipment and data need protecting from risks such as physical damage, theft, unauthorised interference and viruses

- Computer viruses can be a serious problem. The best solution is to keep anti-virus software running constantly on your computer and make sure that it is updated at least weekly. Firewalls are essential if the organisation's systems are connected to the internet

- Data that is accidentally deleted can often be recovered, providing the user acts quickly

- Unauthorised access to computers and data can be prevented with security hardware, passwords and simple precautions such as switching the machine off when not in use

- Passwords are a good means of protection but they do not guarantee protection. They can easily be forgotten or be revealed to non-authorised persons. Passwords should be changed regularly, and changed immediately if they are discovered by a non-authorised person

- The Data Protection Act 1998 gives individuals certain rights and it requires organisations that record and use personal information to follow the eight Data Protection Principles

- Copyright law places constraints on whether you can store and reuse information. The creators of a work have an exclusive right to use it, and also have the right to stop others from using the work without their permission

- The Display Screen Equipment regulations cover a number of aspects of healthy, safe and efficient working, such as taking regular breaks and organising your work area

Keywords

Back-up – a copy of data that can be used if something goes wrong with the original file

Copyright – a way of ensuring that the creators of a work have the right to stop others from using the work without their permission

Encryption – disguising or jumbling up data so that it cannot be read without a key to un-encrypt it

Firewall – a piece of software or a hardware device that can deny access to hackers

Hacking – an attempt to gain unauthorised access to a computer system over the internet

Hoax – a false warning usually sent via email

Personal data – information about living, identifiable individuals

Phishing – a hoax in which the sender attempts to acquire sensitive information such as usernames and passwords by pretending to be a trustworthy organisation

Sensitive data – data about an individual that an organisation may not hold without explicit consent

Virus – a piece of software that infects programs and data and replicates itself to other computers

TEST YOUR LEARNING

Test 1

What are the main carriers of computer viruses?

Test 2

How could you reduce the risk of viruses entering your organisation's computers?

Test 3

What action do you think you need to take if you see a message such as this on your screen?

Test 4

If you saw the following message on your screen what option would you click? Explain your answer.

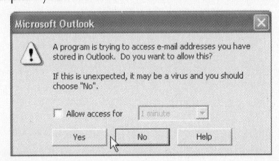

Test 5

When you tell a computer to delete a file, what actually happens, and why may it be possible to recover the file?

Test 6

What are the eight Data Protection Principles?

Test 7

You believe that a credit card company may hold incorrect information about you in its computer files. What are your main rights under the Data Protection Act 1998?

Test 8

Copyright legislation prevents you from re-using other people's ideas. True or False? Explain your answer.

Test 9

If you don't have a copy of the latest version of Microsoft Office on your home computer, is it allowable to take home the program disks from your organisation and install them at home? Explain your answer.

Test 10

How long must most accounting data be retained for? Why?

Test 11

What aspects of your working area are covered by the VDU regulations besides the screen itself?

Test 12

What is encryption and when is it particularly important?

chapter 2:
SAGE – PART 1

chapter coverage 📖

You will be required to prove your competence in the use of computerised accounting software by completing an assessment. Assessments are likely to include a series of exercises, for example entering customer and supplier details, posting transactions such as journals, invoices and credit notes, and obtaining reports and print-outs.

This chapter explains how you might complete the hands-on computerised accounts parts of an assessment. It is by no means a comprehensive guide to computerised accounting.

The illustrations in this chapter and the next chapter are from Sage Instant Accounts, which is just one of many packages that you might use. We use a Sage package because these are popular amongst small/medium-sized businesses in the UK, and with colleges for training purposes.

There are a large number of illustrations in this chapter, so don't be put off if it seems long – it should be relatively quick and easy to work through.

The topics covered in this chapter are:

- ✍ Accounting packages
- ✍ Assessments
- ✍ Company data and the general (nominal) ledger
- ✍ Customer and supplier data
- ✍ Journals
- ✍ Entering invoices
- ✍ Help!

ACCOUNTING PACKAGES

Accounting packages range from simple 'off the shelf' analysed cash book style packages to heavy-duty Enterprise Resource Management systems used in large organisations. Very large organisations often have a system that has been built specifically for them, made up of components from a variety of software suppliers, or written for them on a one-off basis.

Obviously, we cannot even begin to cover the vast range of available packages, but we can illustrate the features of a typical package, and the most popular one in the UK among small- to medium-sized businesses is Sage.

Sage produces a variety of accounting packages and this book deals with Sage Instant Accounts. The illustrations in this chapter are taken from version 18. In the remainder of this chapter we will just use the word 'Sage' to refer to Sage Instant Accounts.

Hands-on

The illustrations in this Workbook are taken from Sage.

Sage upgrade their software regularly. However, many features and functions remain the same from version to version. Some training centres may use different Sage packages or different versions of Sage. The different Sage packages for small and medium sized businesses are based on common principles and are very similar in their operation when it comes to performing the tasks included in this Workbook. Some screens and menus may appear slightly different depending on the age or version of the product you are using, but you should be able to work your way through the tasks.

If possible we strongly recommend that you sit at a computer equipped with a version of Sage as you read through this chapter. Most of the activities assume that you are doing this and can complete the tasks we describe as you go along.

Finding your way about: terminology

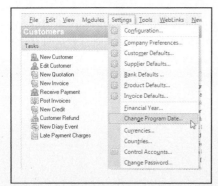

We'll assume that you know what we mean when we say 'menu' and 'button', but there may be some other terms that you are not sure of, so here is a quick guide. In this chapter we will use bold text when referring to something that you will see on screen, such as a button or a menu or a label beside or above a box. For example we might say 'click on the **Settings** menu and choose **Change Program Date**'.

Whilst you can use the buttons on the toolbars as your main starting point it is useful to familiarise yourself with the Settings and Modules buttons as the content of these rarely change although the layout and position of the buttons can vary between different versions. Here is the main toolbar that you can see at the bottom left of the screen when you open up Sage Version 12 or later, with the **Customers** button highlighted.

When the **Customers** button is highlighted, the following toolbar appears at the top of the screen.

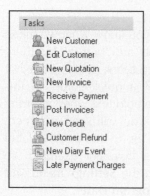

Also, a list of customer-related tasks appears at the top left. Some of the top line of buttons and some of those on the left duplicate actions.

Most of what you do involves you making entries in 'fields' – for example the **A/C** field and the **Date** field in the next illustration.

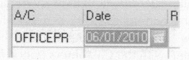

Sometimes you need to select a 'tab' to view the part of the program we refer to. For instance in this example the **Activity** tab is selected.

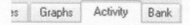

Finally, make sure that you know where the **Tab** key is on your keyboard (usually above the Caps Lock key) and also that you are aware of the function keys (**F1**, **F2** and so on, usually along the top). The **Esc** key is also very useful for closing windows quickly.

Defaults

Computerised packages make extensive use of 'defaults', which are the most common entries. When you start entering data you will often find that Sage has done some of the work already, using the default options that would normally be chosen. This saves a great deal of time, but you should always glance at the default entries in case they are not the ones you want. This will become clearer as you start using the package.

Screen captures and screen prints

You might be asked to print a screen or you might want to do this to record a problem.

To take a screen capture of an entire screen, on your keyboard press **Print Screen** or **PrtScn**. To capture the active window only press **Alt + Print Screen** or **ALT + PrtScn**.

These actions capture the screen or window onto the computer's clipboard. The image can then be pasted into another application (using **CTRL + V**) such as *Word* from where the image can be printed. **Please ensure you are able to complete this action as it is an assessment requirement.**

ASSESSMENTS

Your AAT assessment will involve a number of practical tasks that test your competence in the assessment criteria.

Before you start...

Before you start, you should find out from your assessor what the arrangements are for:

- Opening the accounting package and logging in, if necessary.
- Changing any overall company details or settings, if required.
- Creating new accounts as necessary.
- Posting transactions and completing other assessment tasks.
- Making your own back-ups.
- Printing out or exporting your work.

Backing-up and restoring

We've already discussed the importance of back-ups in computing in general and, of course, this also applies to the data in your accounting system.

Unlike a program such as a word processor or a spreadsheet, when you make an entry in Sage, that data is saved immediately. This means that you can post an invoice, say, then close down the program. Your invoice will not be lost: it will still be there when you next open the program.

In Sage a back-up is created by clicking on the **File** menu (top left of screen) and choosing **Backup**. Fairly logical. You'll be asked if you want the program to check your data first, and it is worth doing this occasionally.

Then you will need to choose a name for your back-up file and a location.

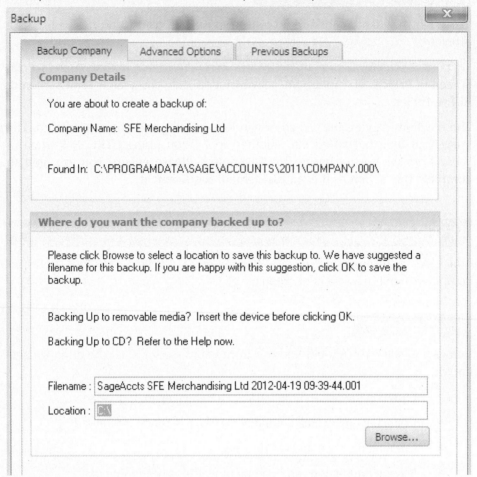

The program suggests a name based on the current date and a number but you can choose any name you like; ask your assessor if there is any particular style of file name that you should use (for instance ASSESSMENT.ABC, where ABC are your initials).

In the preceding example, the back-up will be saved in a folder on a server. Again, you should ask your assessor about the location you should use. Make a note of the location, such as the drive and folder used, so that you will be able to locate the data again quickly.

The **Advanced Options** allow you to choose what to back-up.

Different organisations will have different policies as to what needs to be backed up. Some may require modified Report Files to be included, some may require the Audit Trail History to be included. As a minimum, Data Files must be backed-up.

Backup   ☒

Backup Company	Advanced Options	Previous Backups

File types to include in backup

Type	Included?
Data Files	☑
Report Files	☐
Layout Templates	☐
TMail Database	☐
	☐
	☐
	☐
	☐

☐ Select all file types to include in backup

Restoring data is just as easy: click on **File** and then **Restore** and locate your back-up file.

When you restore from a back-up this will overwrite any data that is currently held in the program's data files, **so take care with this**. If you post a transaction and then restore an old back-up, that transaction will be lost.

You may be asked to restore a back-up before you start an assessment, because this is an excellent way of making sure that everyone starts from the same point, with the same opening balances, the same general (nominal) ledger structure and codes, and so on.

A typical assessment

The following example is based on a sample simulation issued by the AAT (simulations were used before assessments).

Situation

SFE Merchandising is a new business that has been set up by Charlize Veron, one of Southfield Electrical's former marketing staff. Charlize is an expert on store layout and management of inventories (stocks) and she intends to sell her skills and knowledge, on a consultancy basis, to medium and large retailers to help them to optimise their sales.

Charlize has started her new venture as a sole trader and has taken on some of the risk herself. However, SFE Merchandising is part-financed by Southfield Electrical, and may well be acquired by them if this new venture is a success. Initial enquiries have been so promising that Charlize has already voluntarily registered for VAT and intends to run the standard VAT accounting scheme. (Assume the standard VAT rate is 20%).

The business commenced trading on 1 January 2012.

Tasks to be completed

It is now 31 January 2012 and you are to complete the following tasks …

There may be around 20 tasks involving setting up data, entering journals, posting sales and purchase transactions, obtaining print outs and so on.

You will be provided with a series of documents such as invoices, cheques, etc. We'll show you how to deal with all of this in the remainder of this chapter.

You should now have Sage open on your computer and follow through the activities.

Task 1

Preliminary

This exercise starts with a new installation of Sage or a 'clean' company which contains no transactions.

Your college will tell you how to install Sage afresh or from where to restore the clean company.

If you are studying at home and are installing Sage for the first time on a particular PC, follow the on-screen installation instructions for a standard installation – then **go to the New Set Up instructions on the next page**.

If you are studying at home and **have an existing Sage ledger**, you may **create a new installation and a blank ledger** by following the steps below.

- **Make a backup of the existing data if you will require it again in the future**

- Click on the File button along the top menu and select Maintenance

- Click on the Rebuild option and untick all of the options on the left hand side. In some cases you may need to keep the nominal ledger accounts ticked to maintain the Chart of Accounts. This will vary from version to version

- Once the rebuild is complete you will be asked to enter the month and year of the company being worked on. This is given in the scenario. If no year is given use the current year.

- Now go to the settings options and overtype the name of the existing company with that of the new company and change the program date if required to do so

Two important points to note:

- **You will not be required to set up a new company in your real assessment. We cover this here to enable us to create the same starting point in Sage for all students**

- **If installing the program for the first time you will need to know its Serial Number and Activation Key**

New Set Up

The first time you open the package you are presented with a company set-up wizard.

Select the type of data you want to use

Welcome to Sage Instant Accounts

Choose one of the following options:

◉ **Set up your Company Data**
Start using your own company's data.

○ **Open Practice Data**
Practice using the program's features without affecting your company's data. This will start as a blank set of company information.

○ **Open Demonstration Data**
See an example company we have created for you. This includes customer and supplier invoices and payments.

Select the top option to set up your company data and click **OK**.

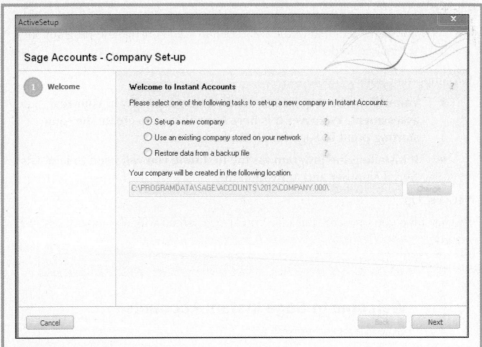

Select **Set-up a new company** and press **Next**.

If your Sage installation does not start at the set-up wizard, you can enter the company information by accessing **Settings** > **Company Preferences** from the menu at the top of the screen.

COMPANY DATA AND THE GENERAL (NOMINAL) LEDGER

Company data

The name and address of the business should then be entered. This information will appear on any documents you produce with the package, such as reports and invoices, so make sure it is accurate and spelled correctly.

Enter all the information given in the screen below. Use the **Tab** key on your keyboard to move between different lines. Alternatively, click on each line, but this will slow you down, so get into the habit of using the **Tab** key to move from field to field (almost all packages work this way). When you have finished press **Next** (each time you complete a new screen you will need to press **Next** to continue – you can also use the **Back** button if you need to re-visit a screen).

Enter Company Details

Company Name :	SFE Mechandising Ltd
Street 1 :	14a Habgood House
Street 2 :	Dagenham Avenue
Town :	Benham
County :	
Post Code :	DR6 8LV
Country :	United Kingdom GB

> After typing a line use the TAB key on your keyboard to move to the next line

Accounts in the general (nominal) ledger

The **general ledger** is the ledger that contains all of the business's income statement (profit and loss) and statement of financial position (balance sheet) accounts. This is also known as the **nominal ledger** and 'nominal ledger' is the term used by Sage.

When a new business is first set up there is a choice between a number of different templates or 'Chart of Accounts' (COA).

The charts provided are tailored towards the type of business. In Sage Instant Accounts 2012 it gives you a choice between a Sole Trader, Partnership and Limited Company. SFE Merchandising is a limited company so you should select this option – **Limited Company**.

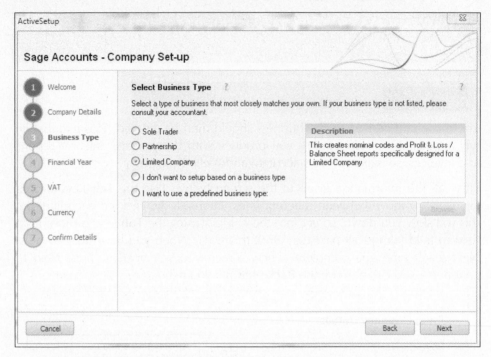

If you are using previous versions of Sage Instant Accounts or you are using Sage Accounts 50 you may be faced with a number of chart of accounts for different types of limited company, similar to that shown below.

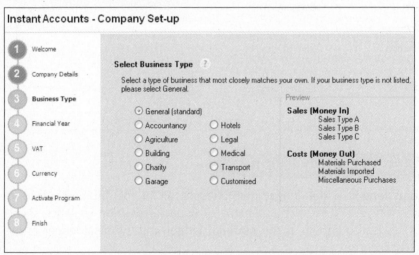

These have accounts tailored for the particular business type.

For example, the 'Hotels, Restaurants and Guest Houses' chart includes sales accounts for 'Restaurant Meals', 'Alcoholic Beverage Sales' and so on.

Many organisations use the 'General' chart, and modify it to suit their needs. If you are faced with the screen above, choose the **General (Standard)** chart of accounts.

Note that you are not confined to using the accounts that you are given by the program when you first set up the company. Certain accounts must always remain because the program will not be able to operate without them – so you will not be able to delete the main bank account, the receivables (debtors) and payables (creditors) control accounts, VAT accounts, and certain other essential accounts. But you can delete any non-essential accounts (so long as you have not yet posted any transactions to them), and you can rename them and add new accounts as required.

Financial year

Set the start of the financial year to January 2012. This can be done either by progressing through the wizard or by accessing **Settings > Financial Year** from the menu.

VAT

The business **is** VAT registered (so select **Yes** in the wizard) and is not registered for cash accounting. Using either the wizard or by choosing **Settings > Company Preferences > VAT** Enter 524 3764 51 as the VAT number.

Enter the standard VAT rate % as 20.00.

Currency

Select **Pound Sterling**, either from the wizard or **Settings > Currency** from the menu.

Activate program

If necessary, activate the program by entering the serial number and activation code supplied with the program or by your college and then click **Finish.**

On clicking Finish you may need to call Sage to fully register your product. The number to call will appear on your screen. Sage should talk you through how to register and how to restart the program having done so.

You are now ready to proceed entering the company's transactions.

New accounts and your assessment

In your assessment you may need to add new nominal ledger accounts to complete your tasks, or you may not. As you work through your assessment, before starting each task check that the accounts you will need are set up. We recommend you create any new accounts required before starting the task the account is needed in.

If the assessment includes a purchase invoice for stationery, for instance, check that there is already an 'Office stationery' overheads account before you start to post the invoice. The tasks may actually ask you to do this. For instance, you may be instructed to work through the invoices provided and write the relevant nominal ledger codes on them.

You can see which chart of accounts has been applied by choosing **Modules > Nominal Ledger** from the menu bar at the top of the screen, or by choosing **Company** from the set of buttons at the bottom left of the screen, then **Nominal Ledger** from the **Links** buttons as shown in the following illustration.

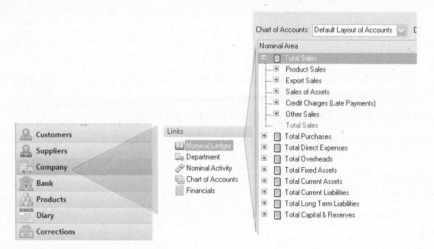

If the chart includes a long list of accounts, you can change it to the format shown above by accessing the **Layout** options at the top right of the screen and choosing **Analyser**.

The chart of accounts, above, has been grouped by type of account. These main headings can be expanded by clicking on the '+' sign next to each heading.

Expand **Total Overheads** and then **Printing and Stationery** and you will see that there is not yet a specific account for Publicity material, so we will create one.

Task 2

Create a new account for 'publicity material'.

Click on the **New** button

and the program will take you through the Nominal Record Wizard. It is possible to set up new accounts without using the wizard, but we strongly discourage this, because it can very easily lead to problems in the way the program handles your new nominal ledger accounts when it is producing reports and financial statements.

On pressing **Next,** the first step is to decide on the **Name** of your new account (overtype 'New nominal account' and choose what **Type** of account it is.

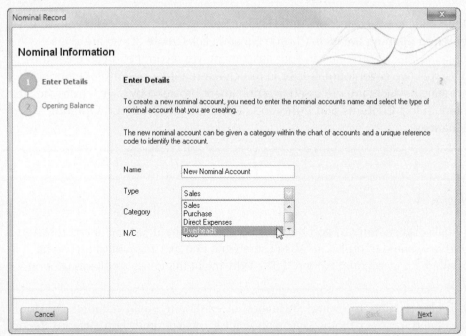

You can further refine the **Category** of account (the options available will depend on the type of account you are setting up – here Printing and Stationery) and choose an account code (**Ref**). In fact the program will suggest a code, depending on the choices you have made so far, and we strongly recommend that you accept this.

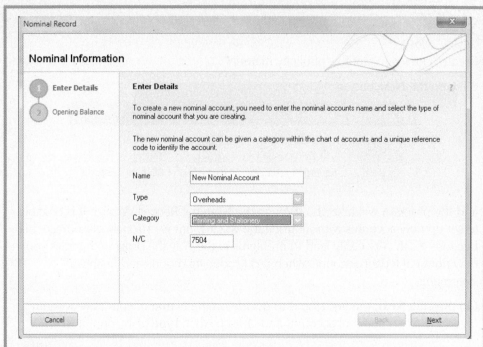

After making your selections and clicking **Next**, you will be asked if you want to **enter an opening balance**. Choose **No** and click **Create**. If you are given opening balances to enter in your assignment, we recommend you enter these as a journal (we cover journals later in this chapter). Other options for entering opening balances are discussed in a document provided by Sage – from the Help menu select **Contents and Index** and navigate to (or search for) **Opening Balances**.

Task 3

Vimal was in a hurry to post a transaction because he'd just had a text message and he wanted to reply. He wasn't sure what nominal account to use, so he created a new account named 'L8R'. Why might this cause problems later on?

It is also possible to change the name of existing nominal accounts. To do this you need to select the account you want to change and then click on **Record**. This brings up a screen showing details of the selected account and you can update the name field. For example you could change 'Sales Type B' to something that is more descriptive of the particular sales to be recorded in that account (eg Overseas Sales).

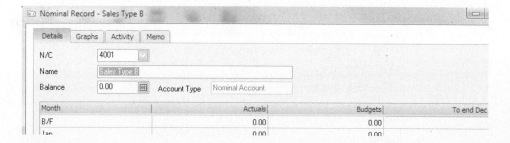

Tax codes

Tax code	Used for
T0	Zero-rated transactions, such as books, magazines, and train fares. (Think of the code as 'T Zero' – then you will never confuse it with the code for exempt transactions).
T1	Standard rate, currently 20%. Some standard-rated items that catch people out are taxi fares (but only if the taxi driver is VAT-registered), restaurant meals, and stationery. You can only reclaim VAT if you have a valid VAT invoice; if not use code T9.
T2	Exempt transactions such as bank charges and insurance, postage stamps, professional subscriptions.
T9	Transactions not involving VAT, for example wages, charitable donations, internal transfers between accounts (for instance from the bank to the petty cash account). Also used if the supplier is not VAT-registered or if you do not have a valid VAT invoice.

There are also codes for transactions with organisations in the EC (outside the UK), because these need to be shown separately on a VAT return, but these are outside the scope of this unit. You may also be aware that there is a reduced rate of 5% for certain things such as domestic electricity, but this does not normally apply to business expenditure.

The above examples cover everything you are likely to encounter in an assessment.

Editing VAT codes and rates

Occasionally new VAT rates such as the 5% rate are introduced or an existing VAT rate is changed. This happened when the rate moved from 17.5% to 20%. This easy to manage on Sage and only takes a few moments. The process is set out below and is for your general information. If you decide to try this out and change the VAT rate using the following steps, **make sure you change it back to 20% before you continue** through the Workbook. Alternatively click on **Cancel** at the end of Step 4 and do not click Save and your changes will not be saved.

Step 1   Click on Settings, and then select Configuration

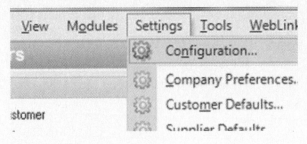

Step 2   Select the **tax codes** tab

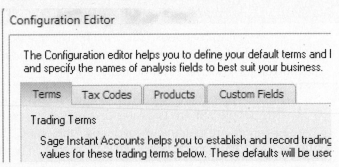

Step 3   In the tax codes tab you will find a list of tax codes. To change an exisiting code it is best to make the changes on the day it begins to affect your company or the nearest trading day after that, highlight the tax code on the list and then click on **Edit**.

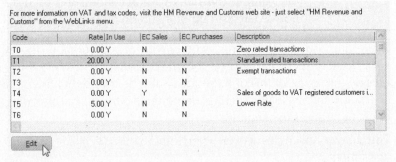

Step 4   The following pop-up screen appears. Simply overtype the existing rate with the new rate (this should be done on the day the rate changes). Once the rate has been updated clicking **OK** makes the pop-up screen disappear and the entry will have been amended in the tax code list. Clicking on **Save** results in the company tax code being updated but you should exit without clicking Save as we want to keep the VAT rate as 20%.

BPP
LEARNING MEDIA

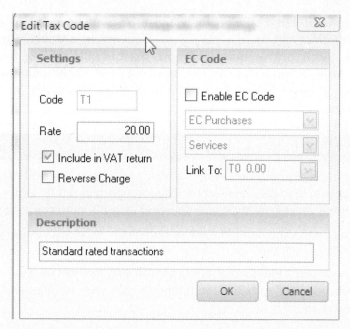

Some companies may prefer to run the older code and newer tax codes concurrently for a short while and in this case a new code will need to be created. To do this you would follow the instructions above but instead at Step Three a code should be selected that is currently unused (such as T3). The the older rate will be entered there, ensuring the **Include in VAT return** box is ticked. Step Four is unchanged.

If in doubt about which Tax code to use when creating new tax codes check with a manager or your accountant for advice as all companies are set up differently.

Trade and non-trade receivables

One thing to note is the Sage package does not make a distinction between trade and non-trade (or 'other') receivables; anyone to whom you grant credit is simply treated as a customer in Sage. (You can assign different types of customers to different categories and/or to different 'departments', but that is beyond the scope of your present studies). Another point to note is that Sage uses UK terminology rather than IFRS terminology and therefore uses the term 'debtors' rather than 'receivables'. Therefore the receivables control account in Sage is named the debtors control account. The AAT have stated that you will **not** need to post non-trade or 'other' receivables so you will not need to use Sage's standard 'other debtors' account.

Important note: From now on we will use the same terminology as Sage uses (ie UK terminology) for the purposes of navigating through Sage. However please be aware of the equivalent terms used in international terminology. A list of these is provided at the front of this Workbook and it is the international terminology that will be used in any questions in tasks in your assessment.

CUSTOMER AND SUPPLIER DATA

Before you can post customer and supplier transactions you will also need to set up accounts in the trade receivables ledger (often referred to as the sales ledger) and the trade payables ledger (often referred to as the purchase ledger).

Once again we recommend that you set up all the accounts you need before you start posting any transactions.

In an assessment (and in real life) you will find the details you need on the documents you have to hand: the business's own sales invoices and its suppliers' purchase invoices.

Codes

The first decision you will need to make is what kind of codes to use. In Sage the default behaviour of the program, if you use the wizard to set up the new suppliers record, is to use the first eight characters (excluding spaces and punctuation) of the full name of the customer or supplier, so if you enter 'G.T. Summertown' as the name the package will suggest that you use the code GTSUMMER.

This is a very clear and easy to use coding system because the code actually contains information about the account to which it refers. If you just gave this customer the code '1' that may be fine when you only have a few customers, but if you have thousands it is most unlikely that you would know who, say, customer 5682 was, just from the code.

The program will not allow you to set up two customers or two suppliers with the same code, so if you had a customer called 'G. T. Summerfield' as well as one called 'G.T Summertown' you would get a warning message suggesting that you use the code GTSUMME1. For this reason many businesses actually introduce numbers into their coding systems. For example, you could use the first five letters of the name and then the numbers 001, 002 and so on for subsequent customers or suppliers with the same first five letters in their name (GTSUM001, GTSUM002, and so on).

Of course, in your work you would use the coding system prescribed by your organisation, but in an assessment you may have a choice. We recommend an alphanumeric system (a mixture of letters and numbers), as this displays your understanding of the need for understandable but unique codes.

Task 4

Do you think it is possible for a customer and a supplier to have exactly the same code? Explain your answer.

Entering the account details

We'll now illustrate setting up a supplier account. Please note that **the process is identical for customers**.

If you click the **Suppliers** button (bottom left of screen) this gives you a new set of buttons.

Note: If you don't see the labels (New, Record, Activity...) under each button then go to **Tools > Options** and tick **Show Text Labels** in **Toolbar**. If on clicking the **Supplier** button you see a graphic like the following, you can change the view to the buttons shown above by clicking on **Change View** and then selecting **Suppliers**.

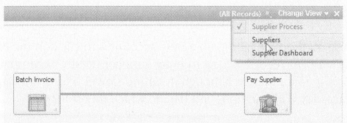

To set up a new account you can click on **Record** and enter as many details as you have available. The details will be found on the supplier invoice. If the invoice shows an e-mail address, for instance, be sure to type it in, even though you may not have e-mail addresses for other suppliers. If you cannot find the relevant field try moving from tab to tab to find the field you want. Most information is entered in the first three tabs (Details, Defaults and Credit Control). Take care with typing, as always. When you are happy that everything is correct click on **Save** and a blank record (like the one shown below) will now appear ready for you to enter the next record. Always remember to click **Save** after entering each supplier and when you are finished click on **Close**.

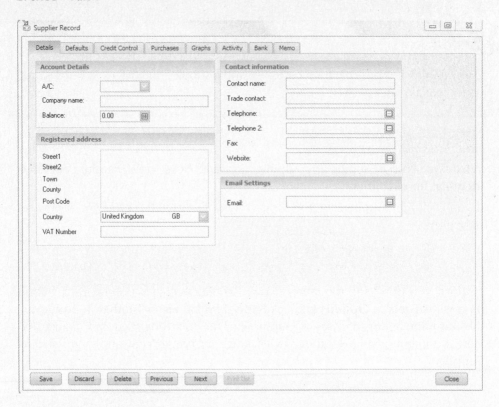

An alternative method for setting up a new account is to click on the **New** button and use the supplier record wizard to enter supplier details. Some people prefer to do this in the first instance although it can be slower and is not often used in the workplace. Try both methods and decide which is best for you.

Task 5

Set up a supplier account based on the following details taken from the heading of an invoice. Decide on an appropriate coding system yourself.

McAlistair Supplies Ltd
52 Foram Road
Winnesh
DR3 5TP
Tel: 06112 546772 Fax: 06112 546775
E-mail: sales@mcalisupps.co.uk
VAT No. 692 1473 29

If you use the wizard, Don't put anything in for any other data, except for clicking on 'Terms Agreed' in the 'Additional information (2)' screen.

Remember to **Save** the new account

You will now see that McAlistair Supplies is now listed as a supplier in the main supplier window. Selecting McAlistair from the list then clicking on **Record** will bring up the following screen:

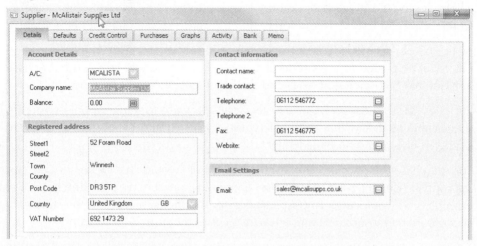

If you see the following message:

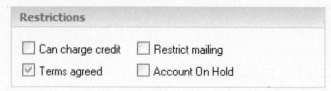

then click on the Credit Control tab for this record.

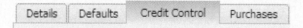

Put a tick in the appropriate checkbox at the foot of the screen, and then save the record. This is simply something Sage requires in order for you to continue entering data for this supplier/customer.

Customer and supplier defaults

By default, when you set up a new customer account the transactions you enter will be posted to the Debtors Control Account (debit gross amount), the Sales Tax Control Account (credit VAT amount) and the Sales Account (credit net amount).

Again, by default when you set up a new supplier account the transactions you enter will be posted to the Creditors Control Account (credit gross), the Purchase Tax Control Account (debit VAT) and the Purchases Account (debit net).

For sales, this is most probably exactly what you want to happen, unless you are specifically instructed that different types of sales should be posted to different sales accounts in the nominal ledger.

For purchases, however, for each supplier it would be better to set an appropriate default for the expense depending on the type of purchase. For example you would want to post a stationery supplier's invoices to the stationery account, but an insurance company's invoices to the insurance account.

To change the defaults, just open the supplier record and click on the **Defaults** tab.

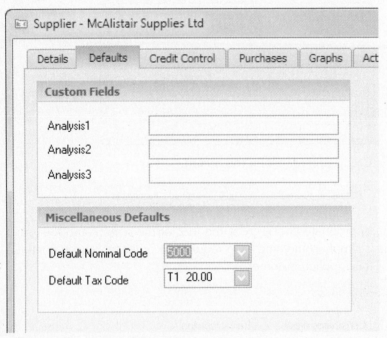

In the box labelled **Default Nominal Code** you can set the nominal ledger account to which all transactions with this supplier will be posted, unless you specify otherwise when you actually post a transaction. To see a list of all available accounts click on the arrow  at the right of the box or just press the F4 key on your keyboard. For example, we may wish to set the default for McAlistair Supplies to Publicity Material.

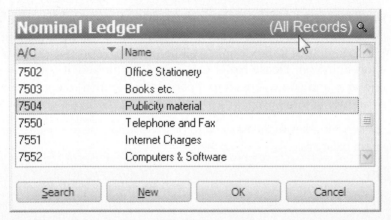

We could scroll down the list to the Publicity Material account created earlier (account 7504). If you need a new nominal account to post to, you can set one up from this screen - but we recommend using the wizard, as mentioned earlier.

Task 6

Open McAlistair Supplies Ltd suppliers record and set the default nominal code to 7504, Publicity Material.

Remember to **Save** this change.

JOURNALS

If you are setting up a new business the first entries you are likely to make will be done via a journal, to set up any opening balances. As a bare minimum there will probably be some money in the business bank account, and this needs to be reflected in the accounts.

To post a journal in Sage click on the **New Journal** button under **Tasks**, at the top left of the screen, shown when **Company** is chosen.

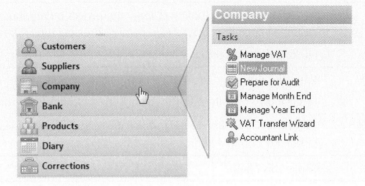

This new journal screen looks reassuringly similar to a journal slip in a manual system, but all you need to do in a computerised system is fill in the slip and click on **Save**. All the entries to the 'books' will then be made in one go without any further effort from you. **Please Note:** Once saved or 'posted' it is not possible to correct a journal and you will need to input another journal to correct any errors so check carefully before saving.

Let's suppose your assessment asks you to post the following journal, to set up the opening cash balances.

DEBIT	Bank	2,750.00	
DEBIT	Petty Cash	250.00	
CREDIT	Ordinary Shares		3,000.00

The Nominal Ledger journal input screen is shown below.

The table below explains what to do as you work through each entry field, in the order in which the TAB key will take you through them.

SCREEN ITEM	HOW IT WORKS
Reference	Type in the journal slip number you are given, if any. Journals should be numbered consecutively, so you may need to check to find out the number of the previous journal. If this is the first ever journal, choose your own coding system and make sure it has room for expansion. For example "J001" allows for up to 999 journals in total.
Date	By default this field (box) will show the program date, but you should change it to 1/1/12 (see below). Pressing the F4 key, or clicking the ▣ button will make a little calendar appear.
N/C	Enter the nominal ledger code of the account affected, or press F4 or click the ⌄ button to the right of this field to select from a list.
Name	This field will be filled in automatically by the program when you select the nominal code.
Ex. Ref	Leave this blank.

SCREEN ITEM	HOW IT WORKS
Details	Type in the journal narrative. In the second and subsequent lines you can press the F6 key when you reach this field, and the entry above will be copied without you needing to retype it. This can save lots of time.
T/C	The VAT code, if applicable. For journals this will almost always invariably be T9 (transaction not involving VAT).
Debit/Credit	Type in the amounts in the correct columns. If it is a round sum, such as £250 there is no need to type in the decimal point and the extra zeros.

It is not possible to post a journal if it does not balance.

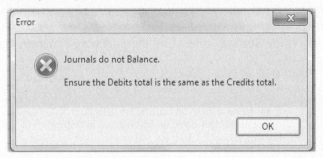

Task 7

Enter the journal shown on the previous page. Date it 1/1/12 and give a reference of JVI and tax code (T/C) 9. Enter 'Initial capital' in the details field. **Save** then **Close** the journal window.

If you click on **Company** you should see that 3,000 is listed against Total Current Assets and 3,000 listed against Capital & Reserves.

The importance of dates

By default, Sage sets the date of transactions to the current date according to your computer, but this may not be the date you want to use, especially if you are sitting an assessment.

It is vitally important to enter the correct date when you are using a computerised system, even if you are only doing a practice exercise, because the computer uses the date you enter in a variety of ways – to generate reports such as aged debtors reports, to reconcile VAT, and so on.

If you attempt to enter a date outside the financial year, you will see a warning such as the following.

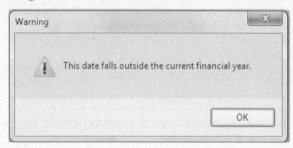

However, if you enter an incorrect date that falls within the financial year, Sage will allow you to do this.

The best way to avoid this kind of error, especially when undertaking an assessment, is to use the facility to set the program date before you enter any transactions. Select the **Settings** menu and then **Change Program Date**.

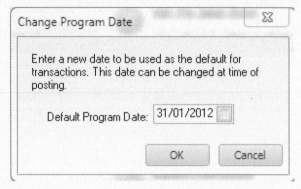

If you are doing an assessment we recommend that you set the program date to the last day of the month for which you are supposed to be posting transactions. That way you can never go seriously wrong.

Once you set the program date Sage will use it as the default date until you change it again or shut down the program. This has no adverse effect on any other programs you may be using and even within Sage the date will revert to the computer clock date the next time you use the program. Note that you will need to set the program date again if you shut down and then restart the program.

Task 8

Change the program date to 31 January 2012 and check that you have done so correctly by looking at the foot of the Sage screen.

Then close down the program (**File > Exit**). You should back-up your data when prompted to do so, using a file name that includes your own initials. You may need to ask your lecturer or manager where you should save the back-up file.

ENTERING INVOICES

You may be feeling that you have been working hard but not actually accomplished much yet! This is one of the few off-putting things about accounting packages: it can take quite a while to set everything up properly before you can really get started.

If you are feeling frustrated, just remember that you only have to set all these details up once. In future, the fact that all the data is available at the touch of a button will save you a vast amount of time, so it really is worth the initial effort.

Purchase invoices

Purchase invoices are created by your suppliers, whereas sales invoices are documents you create yourself. That means that it is usually simpler to enter purchase invoices so we'll deal with those first.

Having opened Sage, click on the **Suppliers** button (bottom left of screen) and then on **Invoice** on the Suppliers toolbar (change view to **Suppliers** if necessary).

As always, you can use the **TAB** key to move between different parts of the screen.

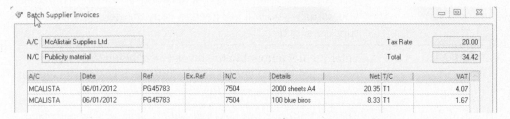

You can enter a number of different invoices from different suppliers on the same screen, and you can enter each line of an invoice separately. Obviously, you would need to do this if the invoice is for a variety of items that need to be coded to different nominal accounts.

To repeat the same entry in consecutive lines just press the **F6** key on your keyboard when you reach the appropriate field. For example, most of the second line in the illustration on the previous page can be entered like this, since the details are mostly the same.

The following table explains what to do as you tab through each entry field. Pay particular attention to the **Net**, **T/C** and **VAT** fields.

SCREEN ITEM	HOW IT WORKS
A/C column	Select the supplier account from the drop down list (press the F4 key to see this, or click on the  button). The A/C box at the top left of the screen will show the full name of the supplier you select, so you can check to make sure you have the right one.
Date	The program date will be entered by default, but you can change this if you wish. Press F4 to see an on-screen calendar.
Ref	Type in the supplier's invoice number.
Ex. Ref	Leave this blank.
N/C	This will show the default code for this supplier (the N/C box at the top left of the screen will show the name of this account). If you need to change it press F4 or click the button to see a list of nominal ledger accounts.
Details	Type in a brief but clear description of the item and be sure that your description will be understood by someone other than you. Usually you will just need to copy the description on the supplier's invoice.
Net	Enter the net amount of the invoice, excluding VAT. If the invoice has several lines you can enter each line separately but you should use the same Ref for each line.
	The button in this field will call up an on-screen calculator.
	Alternatively, type in the gross amount and press the **F9** key on your keyboard (or click Calc Net).
T/C	The VAT code, as explained earlier. Type in or select the appropriate code for the item.
VAT	This item will be calculated automatically, depending on the tax code selected. Check that it agrees with the VAT shown on the actual invoice. You can overtype the automatic amount, if necessary. You may need to do this if the VAT is affected by settlement discount.

When you have entered all the invoice details you post them simply by clicking on **Save**. This will post ALL the required accounting entries to the ledgers.

Task 9

Post an invoice from McAlistair Supplies dated 6 January 2011 for 2000 sheets of A4 paper (net price: £20.35) and a box of 100 blue promotional biros (gross price: £10.00). The invoice number is PG45783. **Save** and **Close**.

Write down the total amount of VAT, as calculated by the program.

£_____

I don't believe it!

The first time you do this you will probably not quite believe that double entry to all the ledgers can be so incredibly easy. Check for yourself by looking at the individual accounts.

To check the nominal ledger click on the **Company** button (bottom left of the screen) then on **Nominal ledger** in the links section (alternatively you can click on the **Modules** menu and choose **Nominal ledger**).

Depending on which type of transaction you posted you should then select either the Debtors Ledger Control Account or the Creditors Ledger Control Account by expanding Total Current Assets or Total Current Liabilities using the '+' signs. Having selected the account you want, you should then click on **Record**.

Choose the **Activity** tab and you will see something like this.

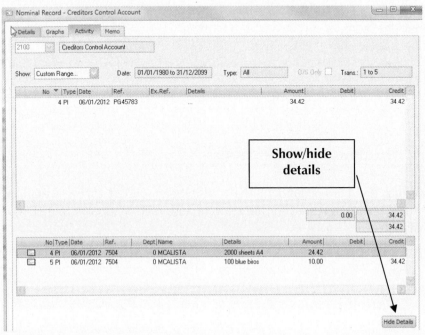

You can also click on the expense account in the nominal ledger and see the activities for that account.

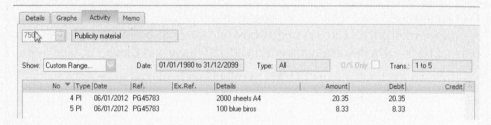

VAT was dealt with by a debit to the Purchase Tax Control Account.

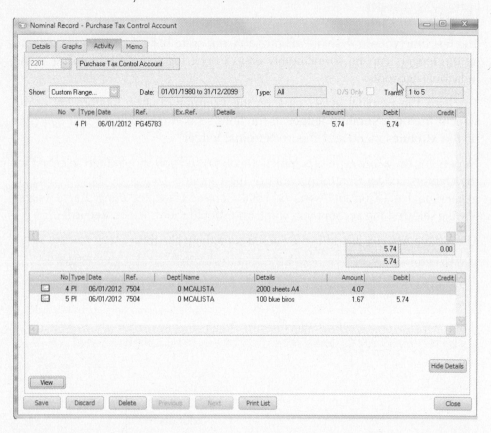

To check that the correct amounts have also been posted to the subsidiary ledger, simply open the record for the relevant customer or supplier and choose the **Activity** tab.

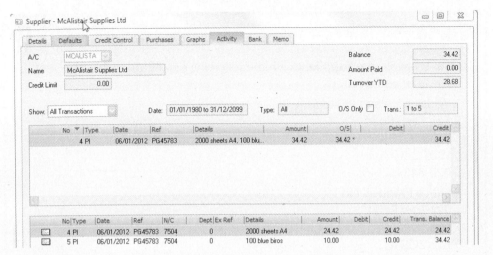

Finally, if you just want a quick look at the transactions you've posted, click on the **Modules** menu then select **Financials**, (or press the **Company** button then **Financials** in **Links**). This will result in you being shown a list of transactions, numbered in the order in which you posted them. This can be very useful on certain occasions, for instance, if you can't remember the reference number of the last journal you posted you can quickly check using this screen.

No ▼	Type	Account	Nominal	Details	Date	Ref	Ex.Ref	Net	Tax	T/C	Paid	Amount Paid	Bank
1	JD		1200	Initial capital	01/01/2012	JVI		2750.00	0.00	T9	Y	2750.00	N
2	JD		1230	Initial capital	01/01/2012	JVI		250.00	0.00	T9	Y	250.00	-
3	JC		3000	Initial capital	01/01/2012	JVI		3000.00	0.00	T9	Y	3000.00	-
4	PI	MCALISTA	7504	2000 sheets A4	06/01/2012	PG45783		20.35	4.07	T1	N	0.00	-
5	PI	MCALISTA	7504	100 blue biros	06/01/2012	PG45783		8.33	1.67	T1	N	0.00	-

Sales invoices if no invoice is produced

Some businesses create sales invoices using a different system from their accounts package – a word processor, for instance.

If that is the case then sales invoices are entered in exactly the same way as purchase invoices. To do this, click on **Customers** then **Invoice** and enter the invoices in a batch.

Sales invoices if the system creates the invoice

If you use your accounting package to produce printable invoices, you begin by clicking on **Customers** and then the **New Invoice** button under **tasks**.

Task 10

(1) Set up two more **suppliers** with the following details (using the new supplier wizard if you wish).

Widgets Unlimited Ltd
123 High Road
London
W23 2RG
020 8234 2345

Office Products Ltd
321 Low Road
London
E32 2GR
020 8432 5432

(2) Process the purchase of:

(a) 10 widgets (material purchased) from Widgets Unlimited Ltd for a total net cost of £80. Invoice number WU4474, dated 8 January 2012.

(b) A computer (office equipment) from Office Products Ltd for a net cost of £800. Invoice OP1231, dated 10 January 2012.

Both purchases attract VAT at the standard rate.

Task 11

(1) Set up a new **customer** with the following details (using the new customer wizard if you wish).

Alexander Ltd
501 Dart Road
Leeds
LS12 6TC
0113 2454 3241
info@alexander.co.uk

30 days' credit (payment due days)
All other fields can be left blank but tick the **terms agreed** option

(2) Post the following two invoices (remember, you have to use '**Save**' to post them) to this customer:

(a) Invoice 1: Product: 10 widgets at a selling price (net) of £20 each. VAT to be charged at standard rate. Date 15 January 2012.

(b) Invoice 2: Service: Advice on widgets, at a fee of £50. VAT to be charged at standard rate. Date 25 January 2012.

(3) Change the name of the nominal ledger account 'Ordinary Shares' to 'Capital'

Task 12

Preview a trial balance at this stage. Select **Company > Financials > Trial > Preview**, set month period to January 2012.

Date:			Page:	1
Time:				

SFE Mechandising Ltd

Period Trial Balance

To Period: Month 1, January 2012

N/C	Name	Debit	Credit
0030	Office Equipment	800.00	
1100	Debtors Control Account	300.00	
1200	Bank Current Account	2,750.00	
1230	Petty Cash	250.00	
2100	Creditors Control Account		1,090.42
2200	Sales Tax Control Account		50.00
2201	Purchase Tax Control Account	181.74	
3000	Capital		3,000.00
4000	Sales - Products		200.00
4001	Sales - Services		50.00
5000	Materials Purchased	80.00	
7504	Publicity material	28.68	
	Totals:	4,390.42	4,390.42

Now take a second backup.

Credit notes

Supplier credit notes are posted in exactly the same way as supplier invoices except that you begin by clicking on **Supplier** and then the **Credit** button, instead of the Invoice button. The entries you make will appear in red, as a visual reminder that you are creating a credit note.

Customer credit notes can be posted in this way too, if no printed credit note is required. If you do want something you can print you can click on **Customers**, and choose **New Credit** from the tasks section. The procedure is then exactly the same as for a printed sales invoice.

HELP!

Help in Sage

If ever you are unsure about how to perform a task in Sage, take a look in the built-in Help feature. Help is accessed via the menu, or by pressing the F1 key.

We recommend you explore all of options shown under the Help menu. Selecting **Tutorials** allows you to access a number of useful guides on how to perform common tasks.

To search for a help on a specific topic, from the Help menu select **Contents and Index**.

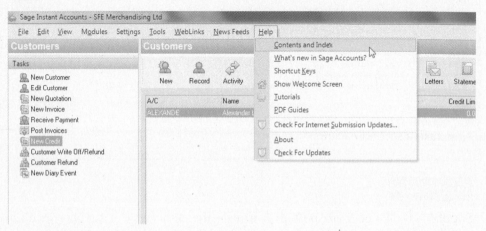

Then, use the Search tab to find the topic you want help on. Experiment with this, the ability to find out how do something yourself could come in handy in your work and in your assessment.

Help from your manager and others

Whenever you are unsure about what to do, or are faced with an error message you are unsure about, the golden rule is **ask for help or advice**.

Don't ignore error messages. If possible, have your manager or someone more senior look at the message immediately and advise you what action to take. If you need to provide details to someone if they can't get to your screen to view it, take a screen print for them.

CHAPTER OVERVIEW

- Accounting packages ange from simple bookkeeping tools to more complex packages. Sage's products among are the most popular packages in the UK

- Assessments may involve setting up new customer and supplier accounts, posting journals, invoices, payments and receipts, and producing printouts or other types of output

- It is essential to make sure that you are posting transactions to the correct financial year

- New nominal ledger accounts can be set up using the accounting package's 'wizard'

- VAT is dealt with by assigning the correct code to a transaction

- New customer and supplier accounts should be given consistent and meaningful codes

- Using the keyboard shortcuts may help you when you are entering data into Sage. The Tab key, the Esc key and the function keys (eg F4 and F6) can often speed up your work

- Familiarise yourself with the Help feature, it could come in handy both in your work and in your assessment

- Never ignore error messages, ask for help or advice from your manager

Keywords

Activity – the transactions that have occurred on an account

Back-up – a copy of a file created in case the original is lost or damaged

Chart of accounts – a template that sets out the nominal ledger accounts and how they are organised into different categories

Defaults – the entries that the accounting package expects to normally be made in a particular field

Field – a box on screen in which you enter data or select from a list (similar to a spreadsheet cell)

General ledger – the ledger containing the income statement (profit and loss) and statement of financial position (balance sheet) accounts

Nominal ledger – the term Sage uses for the ledger containing the income statement (profit and loss) and statement of financial position (balance sheet) accounts

Program date – the date Sage uses as the default for any transactions that are posted (the default may be overwritten)

Restore – the process of overwriting the data currently held in the program with back-up data

Tax code – Sage's term for the code to be used to calculate VAT

TEST YOUR LEARNING

Test 1

What is a 'field' in an accounting package?

Test 2

What do you understand by the term 'default'?

Test 3

Why do you think accounts codes are important in accounting packages?

Test 4

Before you shut down an accounting package it is essential to save your work. True or False? Explain your answer.

Test 5

What happens when you restore a back-up file?

Test 6

When is it not possible to change the financial year of an accounting package?

Test 7

Why is it important that details such as company name and address are entered with no mistakes or typing errors?

Test 8

What is a chart of accounts?

Test 9

In an accounting package there will usually be codes for at least four different types of transactions. What are these types?

Test 10

What must be done before a supplier credit invoice can be posted?

Test 11

How would a supplier invoice be assigned to the correct nominal ledger account?

Test 12

If you attempt to post a journal that does not balance the difference will be posted to the suspense account. True or False? Explain your answer.

Test 13

Why is it so important to enter the correct date for a transaction?

Test 14

If a purchase invoice has five separate lines should these be posted individually or is it sufficient just to post the invoice totals.

chapter 3:
SAGE – PART 2

---

chapter coverage 📖

The topics covered in this chapter follow on from where you should have reached in Chapter 2.

The subjects covered in this chapter are:

✎ Payments and receipts
✎ Bank reconciliations
✎ Print-outs and other types of output
✎ Credit control
✎ Error detection and correction
✎ Month-end procedures

PAYMENTS AND RECEIPTS

Your assessment may include details of payments and receipts to enter into the accounts – including both cheques that you have sent to suppliers and cheques received from customers.

Take care that you know which is which. If it is a cheque that you have paid out to a supplier you may only be shown the cheque stub (that's all you would have in practice, after all), such as illustrated below.

Date	....
Payee	....
....
....
....
£	....
	000001

If it is a cheque that you have received from a customer you may be shown the cheque itself.

Lloyds TSB	**30-92-10**
Benham Branch	Date _____
Pay _____	
_____	
_____	
	FOR WHITEHILL SUPERSTORES

You can tell that this is a receipt because the name below the signature (here Whitehill Superstores) will be the name of one of your customers.

Alternatively, you may be shown a paying-in slip that may include receipts from several different customers.

Cheques etc.			Brought forward £			£50		
						£20		
						£10		
						£5		
						£2		
						£1		
						50p		
						20p		
						Silver		
			Whitehill	1468	75	Bronze		
			Superstores			Total Cash		
						Cardnet		
			G T				3818	75
			Summerfield	2350	00	Cheques etc.		
Carried forward £			Carried forward £	3818	75	Total £	3818	75

Date	23/01/2010	500001	FOR SFE MERCHANDISING	06325143

Supplier payments

When you pay a supplier it is important to allocate your payment to invoices shown as outstanding in the purchase ledger. Sage makes this very easy.

There are a number of different payments allocations that can occur in both the Sale and Purchase ledger. Usually you will pay most invoices in full or take a credit note in full, however there may be reasons why an invoice may only be partially paid, due to disputes or cash flow problems. These are unsurprisingly know as 'part payments'. Occasionally you may not be able to allocate a payment or receipt because it is for an invoice not on the system or the amount does not match with your ledger. In these cases the payment is recorded against the correct account but not to any particular invoice or credit note and these are known as 'payments on account'.

Discounts can be allowed or received, and a discount field is available to make a note of these amounts.

To post a payment to a supplier click on **Bank** on the main toolbar and then on the **Supplier** button towards the top of the screen (NOT the **Payment** button, which relates to payments not involving suppliers accounts).

You are presented with a screen that looks a little like a blank cheque with drop-down options which allow you to choose the bank account used for the payment and the supplier who is being paid.

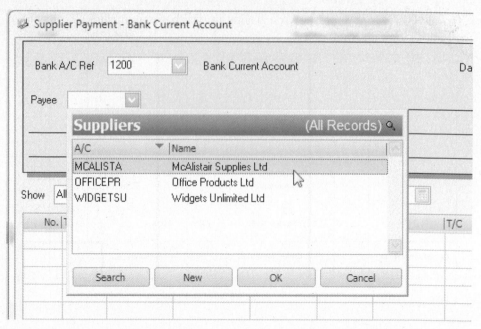

If you choose McAlistair Suppliers Ltd, the next screen completes some of the cheque, and the bottom half of the screen shows details of outstanding invoices.

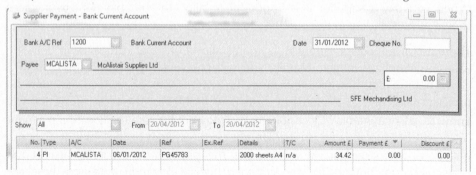

The following table explains the quickest way to post a payment to a supplier. Press Tab to move from one field to the next.

SCREEN ITEM	HOW IT WORKS
Payee	Select the code for the supplier you want to pay
Date	The program date will be entered by default, but you can change this if you wish. Press F4 to see an on-screen calendar.
Cheque number	Enter this carefully as it will help with bank reconciliations
£ box	Though it might seem odd, leave this at 0.00 when paying an invoice in full as it will automatically be filled in when we update the Payment £ box.

SCREEN ITEM	HOW IT WORKS
	Note: When processing a payment on account or unallocated payment you should enter the amount that will be allocated at a later date. On saving a warning screen will appear advising that you are making a payment on account. Such payments should be allocated as soon as the relevant information or invoice is available.
Payment £	Do not type anything here. Just click on the 'Pay in Full' button at the bottom of the screen. If there are several invoices to pay ensure you click into the payment field of the required invoice.
Discount	Tab past this if there is no discount. However if you do need to process a discount enter the discount amount in the discount field *first* and Sage will calculate the balance to be paid and enter it automatically into the payment field.
Save	This saves to ALL the ledgers.

Using this method the amount of the cheque, shown in the £ box in the top half of the screen, updates each time you click on Pay in Full. The program is also clever enough to write the amount in words.

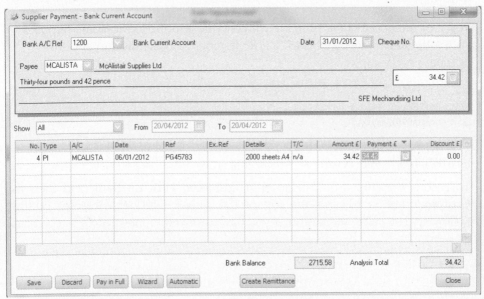

You don't need to pay all the outstanding invoices if you don't want to. You can just click on **Save** when you've paid the ones you want.

This is the quickest way of posting a payment in ordinary circumstances.

There may be times when you don't want to pay invoices in full. For instance, you may decide to pay the supplier in the illustration above only £50, because of some problem with the items supplied. In that case, proceed as follows.

SCREEN ITEM	HOW IT WORKS
Payee	As before
Date	As before
Cheque number	As before
£ box	Though it might seem odd, leave this at 0.00
Payment £	Type the amount you want to pay
Discount	Tab past this
Save	This saves to ALL the ledgers.

A further possibility is that there will be a credit note on the account as well as invoices. **Pay in Full** is the answer to this, too. When you reach the credit note line click on **Pay in Full** and the amount of the cheque will be reduced by the correct amount.

Task 1

Post a payment on 31/01/12 made with cheque 158002 to McAlistair Supplies Ltd for the total of invoice PG45783. Remember to click '**Save**' to effect the posting.

Customer receipts

When you receive money from your customers it is important to allocate your payment to invoices shown as outstanding in the subsidiary ledger.

To record a receipt from an account customer, click on **Bank** and then the **Customer** button towards the top of the screen (NOT the **Receipt** button). Following that, select the customer you have received money from.

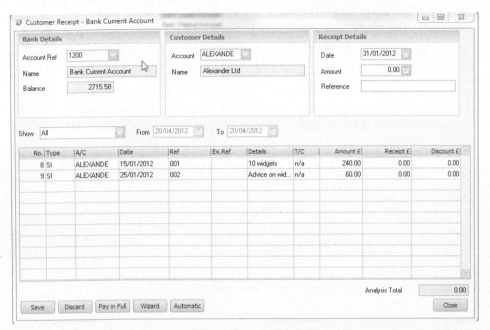

Although this screen looks slightly different from the payment one, it works in exactly the same way, and we recommend that you use it in exactly the same way – in other words, rely on the **Pay in Full** button unless dealing with unallocated payments or 'Payments on Account'.

One important point to remember when posting receipts is that you should use the paying-in slip number (if you have it) for the **Reference**. This makes it much easier to complete bank reconciliations, because typically several cheques will be paid in on a single paying-in slip and the bank statement will only show the total, not the individual amounts.

Task 2

Post a receipt from Alexander for £240. This was paid in using paying-in slip 500001 dated 31 January 2012. You should allocate this against Invoice 1.

Other payments and receipts

Some payments and receipts do not need to be allocated to customers or suppliers. Examples include payments like wages and receipts such as cash sales and VAT refunds.

If your assessment includes transactions like this you should post them by clicking on **Bank** and then **Payment** (or **Bank** and then **Receipt**).

Here's an example of how a loan from the bank might be posted to the accounts (don't carry out the transaction). Use the **N/C** drop-down to find which nominal code to use. Note that transactions like this will often not involve VAT, in which case the **T/C** code to use is T9.

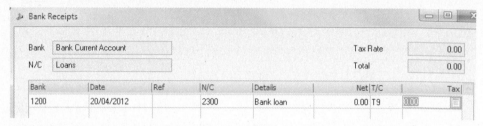

The screen for posting payments such as wages is exactly the same.

Direct debits and standing orders

Many businesses have regular recurring payments, such as rent, set up by standing order or direct debit. It can be easy to forget to post these – especially as some may be monthly, some quarterly and so on.

Although these are recurring payments and Sage does have a recurring payments option **you will only be required to enter direct debits/standing orders as a single transaction in the assessment.**

Therefore, you should enter a standing order or direct debit payment using the method we just looked at in the previous section. For example, if you are presented with a bank statement for the period with a direct debit payment showing for an expense not yet accounted for, you can enter this by clicking on **Bank**, then **Payment** which will bring up the following screen.

The screen above shows how a direct debit payment for rates of £200 could be posted (don't post this transaction now). Standing orders would be posted using the same method.

So really you will use the **Payment** option within **Bank** to post any payments other than:

- those allocated to supplier invoices (using the method we saw earlier)
- transfers between the company's own bank accounts (as there is a separate option for this)

Petty cash

Petty cash transactions are posted in exactly the same way as bank transactions except that you use the Petty Cash bank account rather than the Bank Current Account. As always, take care to use the correct VAT code.

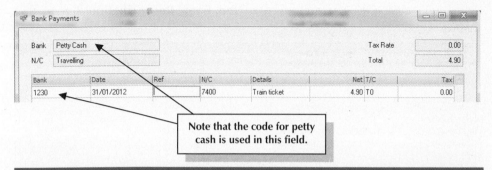

Note that the code for petty cash is used in this field.

BANK RECONCILIATIONS

To access the bank reconciliation screens you need to click on **Bank** and then select the account you want to reconcile. In Sage the default bank current account is account 1200 so you can select this and then click on **Reconcile**. This brings up a statement summary screen.

This screen gives you a first opportunity to enter the statement reference, balance and date and to enter any interest or charges appearing on the statement not yet entered in the records. The ending balance that automatically comes up is the balance on the nominal account, so should be updated to the balance shown on the statement.

Say that the closing bank statement balance is £2,990. That information is entered in the **Ending Balance** box of the Statement Summary screen. If the statement is dated 31/1/2012 that can be entered in the **Statement Date** box.

If you forget to update this balance or any other details, you can also update them in the next screen (the bank reconciliation screen). Adjustments for interest can also be made there.

When you click **OK** you are taken to the **Bank Reconciliation** screen that follows.

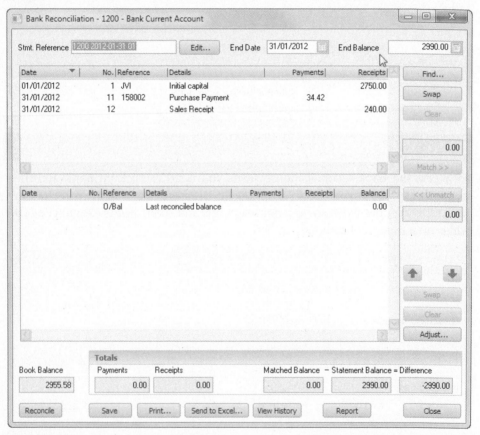

Initially, all cash account amounts are unmatched (you can see the matched balance box at the bottom shows zero), but by looking at the statement, some will be found to appear there also. We can match these items. Say that the initial journal of £2,750 into the bank account and the receipt of £240 from Alexander Ltd are both also on the bank statement.

These can be selected and matched by clicking on the transaction and then on **Match >>** (note if you accidentally match the wrong entry then you can use **<< Unmatch** to go back a step). The statement screen will then look as follows:

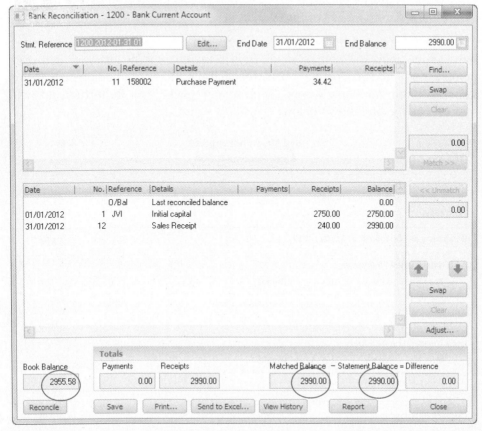

Reconciliation has been achieved! (Matched balance = Statement Balance) and the unmatched item of £34.42 explains the difference between the statement balance of £2,990.00 and the Sage bank current account balance (Book Balance) of £2,955.58.

The fields you enter in the Bank Reconciliation screen are as follows:

SCREEN ITEM	HOW IT WORKS
Date	Set this to the same date as the date of the statement received from the bank (probably the date of the last transaction shown on the statement).
Statement End Balance	Type in the closing balance on the bank statement, using a minus sign if the account is overdrawn.
Difference	This field is updated by the program as you select transactions on screen. The aim is to make this box show 0.00.

Task 3

Carry out the bank reconciliation explained in this section assuming that the closing bank statement balance is £2,990.

Although we look at reports in detail later in the chapter, at this stage it is work pointing out you can generate a bank reconciliation report (a bank reconciliation statement) from the Bank Reconciliation screen. Clicking on **Report** should yield a report like the one shown below.

Date: Time:			**SFE Mechandising Ltd** **Bank Reconciliation**			Page: 1

Bank Ref:	1200		**Date To:**	31/01/2012
Bank Name:	Bank Current Account		**Statement Ref:**	1200 2012-01-31 01
Currency:	Pound Sterling			

Balance as per cash book at 31/01/2012: 2,955.58

Add: Unpresented Payments

Tran No	Date	Ref	Details	£
11	31/01/2012	158002	Purchase Payment	34.42
				34.42

Less: Outstanding Receipts

Tran No	Date	Ref	Details	£
				0.00

Reconciled balance :	2,990.00
Balance as per statement :	2,990.00
Difference :	0.00

Adjustments

Even if you have posted all your transactions correctly there is a good chance that there will be items on the bank statement that you have not included in the accounts. Bank charges and interest are common examples.

Other examples include direct debits and standing orders if you haven't already posted these in another way (such as using bank payments as we saw earlier).

For such items click on the **Adjust...** button on the bank reconciliation screen, select the type of adjustment to bring up the related adjustment screen (for earlier versions of Sage you may be taken straight to a general adjustments screen and will not have the option of also posting supplier and customer payments at this stage).

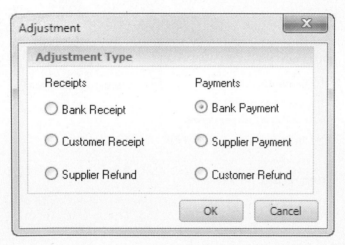

The adjustment screen allows you to enter the amounts and details before Saving. **Note**: For our purposes, **do not** carry out the following adjustment.

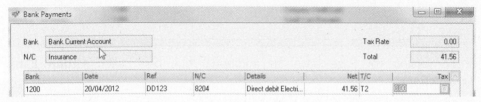

Make sure you use the correct tax code when making adjustments.

Note: On earlier versions of Sage, where you are taken straight to an adjustment screen, you may not be able to use this method to post payments to or receipts from credit suppliers or customers because the subsidiary ledgers will not be updated.

Grouped receipts

As we mentioned earlier, businesses often pay several cheques into the bank on the same paying-in slip and bank statements only show the total of the paying-in slip, not the individual items.

If you use the paying-in slip number as the **Reference** when posting receipts, Sage will allow you to group similar items together when doing a bank reconciliation. This may make it easier to agree them to the bank statement entries.

Within **Bank Defaults** in the **Settings** menu is a tick box called **Group items in Bank Rec**. When this is ticked consecutive transactions of the same type are combined as one item for display in the Bank Reconciliation screen if the reference and the date are the same.

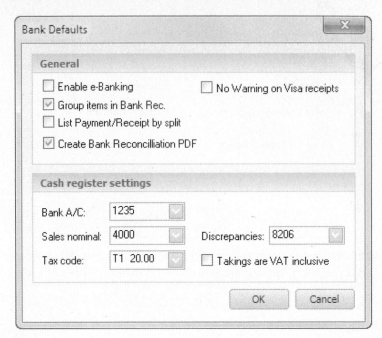

Some versions of Sage have an additional tick box called **Group Bank Transactions**.

If this check box within Bank Defaults is selected, bank transactions (bank payments and bank receipts) with the same reference and transaction date are grouped together within bank activity.

To see the individual transactions that make up the header, you must use the drill-down facility.

If you do not want your bank transactions to be grouped together in, clear the check boxes related to grouping items. When you clear the check boxes, each bank transaction appears on a separate line of the Bank Activity.

PRINT-OUTS AND OTHER TYPES OF OUTPUT

The importance of reports generated by the accounting systems

One of the most important features of an accounting system like Sage is its ability provide a range of useful accounting information very quickly. If transactions are entered correctly in the first instance, then accurate summaries or detailed analysis should be available at the click of a button.

This is very important for both managers and accounts staff who depend on this information to make important decisions. The instant collation of financial information they need means they can make more informed decisions more quickly.

The information needed by each individual in the business will vary depending on their role and the situation they find themselves in. Management may focus more on the summaries to gain an understanding of 'the big picture' while finance staff will typically need to look at the more detailed reports.

To give a simple example of the use of a report by finance staff; the aged receivables analysis can be generated from Sage (as we will see later) and this will show how old each customer balance is. This will alert staff in charge of credit control to those accounts that are overdue and need chasing for payment, without them having to look back at the invoice dates.

The majority of the reports we will look at are usually produced periodically and used to check on the accuracy of the records.

We look at generating a nominal activity report later, which details all the transactions in a period in each account. This can be scanned to identify errors, such as transactions posted to the wrong account by mistake. The trial balance generated by the accounting system may also highlight errors, for example if a suspense account has been set up and not yet been cleared.

We looked at bank reconciliations earlier and checking the related report against the bank statements is an important procedure that should be carried out regularly.

The various reports can also used to gain an overview of different financial areas and as a tool when dealing with customers and suppliers. Areas focussed on might include identifying and dealing with overdue customer invoices (aged receivables analysis), seeing which suppliers due for payment (payables listings) and establishing the cash available to the business to meet its commitments (bank related reports).

Another advantage of accounting systems is that they often contain standard templates of documents the business needs to send to customers and suppliers. For example Sage will use its built in standard templates to produce customer invoices, statements and letters. It does this by populating the standard document with the details previously entered into the accounting system, such as the customer name and address entered when the customer was first set up.

Generating reports

When you have finished entering transactions, the next task in your assessment is likely to be to print out (or generate) some reports. You may also be asked about exporting data or reports to a computer file or direct to e-mail.

Sage offers you a large number of different reports and you can create others of your own if you wish, containing any information you choose. Although the pre-prepared reports that are available in Sage don't all have names that you will immediately recognise from your knowledge of manual accounting systems, rest

assured that everything you are likely to be asked to produce in a assessment can easily be found.

One or two print-outs, such as customer statements, have their own buttons, but in general, to generate and then print a report, you open the part of the program you want a report on and choose the **Reports** button which usually appears on the far right hand side. The report button within **Customers** is found here:

Here's an example of the range of Customers reports that you could print. To get to this screen click on **Customers** then **Reports**. By clicking on each folder you can see the reports available for each category. Remember, Sage uses UK terminology but in your assessment you will be asked for reports named using international terminology. For example you may be asked for an 'aged trade receivables analysis' which will be called an 'aged debtors analysis' in the Sage reporting area.

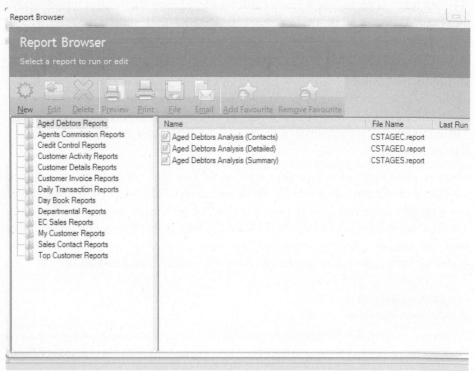

In recent versions of Sage the reports are organised into separate folders by subject, as shown in the illustration. In older versions this screen is laid out slightly differently, listing reports individually in alphabetical order. When you have found your report, select it.

Invoices and statements

Some print-outs, such as invoices and statements, may be intended to be printed on pre-printed stationery. Remember that when you preview these documents on-screen, you will see words and figures on plain paper. This is obvious if you think about it, but we mention it because it surprises some new users.

An extract from a statement displayed on-screen is shown below.

SFE Mechandising Ltd
14a Habgood House
Dagenham Avenue
Benham
DR6 8LV

ALEXAND

Alexander Ltd   31/01/2012
501 Dart Road

Leeds

LS12 6TC

All values are shown in Pound Sterling

15/01/2012	001	Goods/Services	£	240.00			£	240.00
25/01/2012	002	Goods/Services	£	60.00			£	300.00
31/01/2012		Payment			£	240.00	£	60.00

Print-outs in assessments

The following table lists the print-outs you are most likely to be asked for in an assessment with brief instructions explaining how to obtain them in Sage.

PRINT-OUT REQUIRED	HOW TO GET IT	WHICH REPORT TO CHOOSE
Audit trail The audit trail is where Sage stores all of the transactions that you enter. The audit trail is so called because it is a complete record of your transaction activities and is often requested by auditors during their investigations.	Click on **Modules**, select **Financials**, then on the **Audit** button. Note that you can clear the audit trail, (eg as part of the year end routine). This removes fully paid up and reconciled transactions, which speeds up program operation. It is vital to print the audit trail before clearing it.	The **Summary** type of audit trail with **Landscape Output** is the most useful. Just click on **OK** when you are asked for **Criteria** and you will get a list of ALL transactions in the order in which they were posted.

PRINT-OUT REQUIRED	HOW TO GET IT	WHICH REPORT TO CHOOSE
Customer statements	Click on the **Customers** button and then the **Statement** button	*Stat with Tear Off Remit Adv. Individual & All Items*
Bank reconciliation statement	Please refer back to the Bank Reconciliations section of this chapter to see how to generate a bank reconciliation statement.	*Report within the Bank Reconciliation Screen*
	You can also run a retrospective bank reconciliation report by clicking on the **Bank** button, then the **Reports** button and opening the folder **Reconciled Transaction Reports.**	*Retrospective Bank Reconciliation (Detailed)*
	Additionally you can run reports showing reconciled or unreconciled items by clicking on the **Bank** button, then the **Reports** button and opening the relevant folder, ie **Reconciled and/or Unreconciled Transaction Reports**	*For list of reconciled or unreconciled items:* *Bank Statement –* *Bank Reconciled Transactions; or* *Unreconciled Bank Transactions*
Sales and Sales Returns Day Books	Click on **Customers**, then **Reports** and (if necessary) open the folder **Day Book Reports**	*Day Books: Customer Invoices (Detailed)* *Day Books: Customer Credits (Detailed)*
Purchases and Purchases Returns Day Books	Click on **Suppliers**, then **Reports** and (if necessary) open the folder **Day Book Reports**	*Day Books: Supplier Invoices (Detailed)* *Day Books: Supplier Credits (Detailed)*

PRINT-OUT REQUIRED	HOW TO GET IT	WHICH REPORT TO CHOOSE
Journal Day Book	Click on **Company**, then **Reports** and (if necessary) open the **Day Book Reports** folder	*Day Books: Nominal Ledger*
All sales ledger accounts (customer accounts) (showing all transactions within each account)	Click on **Customers**, then **Reports** and (if necessary) open the **Customer Activity Reports** folder	*Customer Activity (Detailed)*
All purchases ledger (supplier) accounts (showing all transactions within each account)	Click on **Suppliers**, then **Reports** and (if necessary) open the **Supplier Activity Reports** folder	*Supplier Activity (Detailed)*
Aged trade receivables/trade payables reports	Click on **Suppliers** or **Customers** as appropriate, then **Reports**	*Choose (and preview) the appropriate aged debtor/creditor reports*
Bank accounts	Click on **Banks**, then **Reports** and choose bank payments, bank receipts etc	*Bank > cash payments* *Bank > cash receipts etc*
All active nominal ledger accounts (showing all transactions within each account)	Click on **Modules**, then **Nominal ledger**, **Reports** and (if necessary) open the **Nominal Activity Reports** folder	*Nominal Activity*
Trial Balance	Click on **Modules** and select **Financials**, then click on the **Trial** button	*Choose Printer when asked about Print Output, unless you only want to preview the report*

Task 4

Set up another customer as follows:

Springsteen Ltd
223 Home Town
Bradford
BD11 3EE

Process an invoice, Invoice 3, to this customer for £600 (net) for 20 Super-widgets, VAT at standard rate, invoice dated 26 January 2012.

Task 5

You notice that on 15 January the bank has debited your account £10 for bank charges (zero rated). Process this to the bank account, debiting the Bank Charges account in the nominal ledger.

On 31 January the bank credits you with £0.54 interest (no VAT). Rather than net this off against Bank interest charges, you decide to set up a new nominal ledger account: Bank interest received, in the Other sales category, account number 4906. Set up the new account and enter the interest received.

Transfers

To transfer between bank accounts (including petty cash) you use the **Transfer** button or the **Record Transfer** option from the appropriate **Task** menu. For example, to transfer £100 from the Bank Current Account to the Petty Cash account select **Bank** from the menu on the bottom left, then **Record Transfer** from the task list.

Task 6

On 23 January, you transfer £100 from the bank account into petty cash and immediately spend:

- £20 on train fares (zero rated for VAT) and
- £10 (gross amount) on coffee mugs for the office (standard rated). The net cost of the cups should be debited to Miscellaneous expenses.

Remember, you can use F6 to repeat entries from the previous line.

Task 7

Extract a trial balance dated 31/01/2012 and back-up your data again.

If you wish you can also preview a statement of financial position (balance sheet) and Income statement (profit and loss account). You will not have to do this in your case study, but they are easy documents to produce and it seems a pity not to have a look!

Modules > Financials > Balance for the balance sheet

Modules > Financial > P and L for the profit and loss account

Your trial balance in Task 19 should look similar to the one below:

Date: Time:	SFE Mechandising Ltd Period Trial Balance		Page:	1

To Period: Month 1, January 2012

N/C	Name	Debit	Credit
0030	Office Equipment	800.00	
1100	Debtors Control Account	780.00	
1200	Bank Current Account	2,846.12	
1230	Petty Cash	320.00	
2100	Creditors Control Account		1,056.00
2200	Sales Tax Control Account		170.00
2201	Purchase Tax Control Account	183.41	
3000	Capital		3,000.00
4000	Sales - Products		800.00
4001	Sales - Services		50.00
4906	Bank interest received		0.54
5000	Materials Purchased	80.00	
6900	Miscellaneous Expenses	8.33	
7400	Travelling	20.00	
7504	Publicity material	28.68	
7901	Bank Charges	10.00	
	Totals:	5,076.54	5,076.54

CREDIT CONTROL

This section deals with:

- Producing statements
- Producing an aged trade receivable analysis and exporting it to a spreadsheet file
- Sending letters to slow-paying customers
- Writing-off an irrecoverable (bad) debt.

Statements are very easy to produce.

Task 8

Make sure the program date is still set at 31/01/2012 (**Settings > Change program date**).

Click on **Customers > Statements** and choose the style of statement and paper size. If you are simply previewing the report, the paper size won't matter, so simply choose the top one offered.

Click on the **Preview** button (or **Generate Report** when in **Preview** mode for previous versions of Sage). Accept the criteria values offered. You will see two statements, one for Alexander Ltd and one for Springsteen Ltd.

Close the statement preview report.

An aged analysis is also easy to produce and this can be printed, previewed or exported.

Task 9

Ensure that the program data is set to 31/01/2012. Go to **Customers > Reports > Aged Debtors Reports**.

From the **Aged Debtors Report** folder select the first report listed.

Use the **Preview button** to generate the report (on older versions of Sage you will need to select the report, ensure preview is selected and click on **Generate Report**).

Accept the criteria offered, and a report will be generated showing all debts as current.

Close the report and set the program date to 31/03/2012. Now generate the report again. You will see the debts are not categorised as Period 2 as they are now two months old (with respect to the program date).

At the top left of the report there is a menu option to **Export** the analysis. Click on that option. This opens another window in which you can choose:

- Where the file will be stored
- The name of the file ·
- What type of file

Choose (or note) where the file will be stored, accept (or change) the name offered and use the drop-down list to specify an Excel file. Finally, locate the file that has just been created and open it with Excel to see its layout and check its contents.

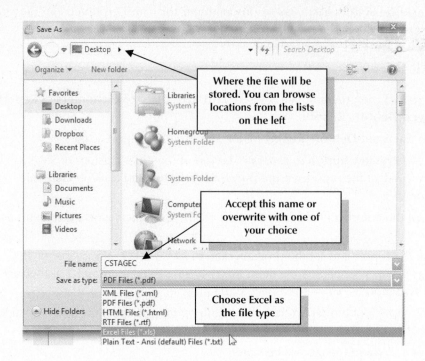

Data can be imported into Sage from sources such as Excel files and database files. This can be a useful way of avoiding the need to manually key in data. The data has to be properly structured to allow the import to go smoothly. Help is provided in Sage 'Help' – search on 'import data'. It is unlikely you would be required to import data in your assessment.

Task 10

Sometimes it is necessary to send letters to customers asking for payment. Follow the steps below to produce payment letters.

First, close any reports that are open.

Then, choose **Customers**, highlight Springsteen, click on **Letters**, choose **Payment Reminder (v.1)**. Generate the report in preview format. You will see a reminder letter addressed to Springsteen.

These letters can be edited (**Edit** button) using the Sage Report Designer or exported and edited in other software.

Unfortunately, despite sending statements and letters, and making phone calls, it's possible that some customers will never pay what they owe – so their debts have to be written-off.

We will now write-off the amount owing from Alexander Ltd, £60.00. In Sage, write-offs (whether specific transactions within an account or whole accounts) are performed using the Write Off Wizard.

Task 11

Click on **Customers> Tasks > Customer Write Off/Refund > Write off Customer Transactions.**

Select the supplier and move on to the next screen where you should click on the invoice and then **Next**. In the next screen enter 'Agreed with chief accountant' as the additional reference before again pressing **Next** (and if applicable **Post**) to complete the write off.

Check the transaction by previewing a trial balance again. You will see a bad debt write-off of £60.00 and that the Debtors Control Account has been reduced to just £720 – Springsteen's debt.

Note also here that the Petty Cash balance is £320. Accessing Activities of the Petty Cash account will show: £250 initial capital, £100 transferred in, £10 and £20 spent. We will return to this in the next activity.

ERROR DETECTION AND CORRECTION

The menu option **Modules > Financials > Verify** allows you to run a routine which attempts to verify data and to report suspected errors, such as duplicated entries.

If you make an error when you are making your entries it is relatively easy to correct.

Errors made when setting up customer and supplier accounts can be corrected simply by opening the relevant record and changing the data.

Errors made when typing in the details of a transaction (references, descriptions etc) can be corrected by clicking on the **File** menu and then on **Maintenance > Corrections**. A list of all the transactions you have posted so far will appear and you can select the one you want to change and click on **Edit Item**. When the record appears you can click on **Edit** and change the details as appropriate.

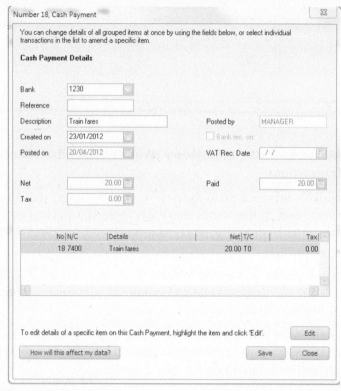

Some corrections that you can make in this way have a bigger effect on the underlying records than others. For example, if you try to change the date or the amounts or account codes for a transaction the program may let you do so, but to guard against fraud it will also post a record of what has been changed, and you will be able to see this if you click on **Modules** and then **Financials**: the correction will show up in red.

Task 12

Let's say that the £20 payment entered in petty cash for a train fare should actually have been £15. We could, of course, make adjustments using a journal entry, but here we will use the correction facility.

In the **File** menu, click on **Maintenance > Corrections**

Look down the list of transactions until you find £20 for the train ticket. Double click on that and enter £15 in the net amount. Save the correction.

Now go to **Bank > Petty Cash** (double click) > **Activity**

You will see that the transaction (probably transaction 17) is now only £15 and the petty cash balance has increased by £5 to £325. However, there is a *memorandum* entry in red stating that £20 has been deleted.

MONTH-END PROCEDURES

Running the month-end procedures allows you to:

- Post prepayments
- Post accruals
- Post depreciation
- Clear the turnover figures. This sets your month to date turnover figures to zero on each customer and supplier record window.

You will not have to set up accruals, prepayments or depreciation in your assessment, but it is important to understand that the month-end procedure allows you to produce monthly accounts, perhaps for comparison with a budget.

The month-end is also a convenient time at which to run the audit trail report (**Modules > Financials > Audit**) which will print out all transactions, and then to clear the audit trail (by selecting **Tools > Period End > Clear Audit Trail**). Clearing the audit trail means that less information has to be held by the system (both live data and back-up data) so that it will operate more efficiently.

To run month-end choose **Company > Manage Month End** (from the task list). This will start up a wizard which guides you through three phases:

Preparation

Post all transactions for the period including recurring entries, set up any pre-payments and/or accruals required, take full account of depreciation in your Fixed Assets Register, optionally reconcile all bank accounts to your bank account statements.

Run month-end

In this phase you create a backup, change your program date to the month-end date, then run the month-end operation to post prepayments, accruals and depreciation, and clear your turnover figures.

Completion

In this third phase you create another backup, then, again optionally, clear your Audit Trail, after which you create another backup.

Starting over

All of us have a bad day sometimes! Occasionally, you may find that you or someone else using the package has made a number of mistakes, perhaps due to a misunderstanding.

If this happens it may well be better to start again rather than trying to correct all the mistakes, possibly making things worse.

To do so, of course, you need to have made a backup of the data as it was before all the errors were made. You can then simply restore the correct data and start posting your new entries again.

This is one of the many advantages of taking regular back-ups!

CHAPTER OVERVIEW

- Payments and receipts should be allocated to outstanding invoices as it is important to know which invoices have been paid

- Bank reconciliations are very important controls in accounting systems and are easily accomplished in Sage

- Good credit control is necessary in many businesses because credit customers are often slow to pay. Sage makes it easy to produce statements, aged debtor analyses and letters to slow payers

- All the printouts that you are likely to require are available as pre-prepared reports

- There are various facilities for error correction, but it is best not to make errors in the first place!

Keywords

Customer – a person or organisation that buys products or services from your organisation

Customer record – the details relating to the customer account, for example name and address, contact details and credit terms

Customer ledger – the collection of customer accounts, also known as the debtors ledger or sales ledger

Supplier – a person or organisation that your organisation buys products or services from

Supplier record – the details relating to the supplier account, for example name and address, contact details and credit terms

Suppliers ledger – the collection of supplier accounts, also known as the creditors ledger or purchases ledger

TEST YOUR LEARNING

Test 1

When you receive a payment from an account customer this is posted from the Bank menu using the Receipt button. True or False? Explain your answer.

Test 2

Once an entry has been made in Sage, the only way to correct it is to use a journal. True or False?

Test 3

The error correction facility wipes out all trace of the original entry. True or False? Explain you answer.

Test 4

Give one reason why the month-end procedure calculates and clears the monthly expense account balances?

Test 5

Transfers between bank accounts should be processed by using the Journal facility. True or False?

Test 6

Taking regular back-ups are unnecessary because computerised accounting packages and modern computer equipment are so reliable. True or False?

ANSWERS TO CHAPTER TASKS

CHAPTER 1

Task 1

One simple rule is don't do anything that you wouldn't do to your TV! We could add some more rules.

- Don't place drinks or other liquids on or near the computer

- Don't place the computer where it can easily be knocked or kicked or where it is subject to strong vibrations or electro-magnetic fields

- Don't move the computer around more than strictly necessary

- If you have to move the machine – even to insert or remove a plug at the back – save and close all current files and switch the machine off first

Task 2

In this example it would be quite all right to choose either of the options 'Permit' or 'Automatically configure internet access' because the program that is trying to access the internet is a tried and trusted email program from Microsoft. This is an example of what may happen when you first install a firewall: it will need some configuration before it knows what internet connections you are prepared to allow without question.

Task 3

Switching off the machine when it is not attended is the simplest method. This prevents casual snoopers from reading files on the screen. Unfortunately, this won't always be possible or desirable, especially if you move around a lot and the machine is needed continuously.

Some users 'disguise' their most sensitive files by giving them uninformative filenames or placing them in unexpected parts of the directory. This is hardly perfect: the chances are that after a while the user will not be able to find the files either! And, in any case, a search based on file content might well reveal the file and its location if the snooper has some inkling of the secrets about you that he or she is trying to discover.

Task 4

Many people feel unhappy about their personal details being retained by commercial organisations. Here are some of the concerns that people have.

- Incorrect details may be entered, causing anything from minor irritation to significant financial problems

- A list or database may be sold to other organisations, who then try to sell various goods and services to the people on it

- 'Personalised' mailings have arrived addressed to someone who has recently died, causing great distress to the surviving partner

Task 5

Personal data may be kept for a number of different reasons. The data most likely to be relevant under the Act is that kept for sales, marketing and promotional purposes. If you believe that you or your department are holding data that should be registered, or you are unsure what can be disclosed to whom, you should discuss the matter with your line manager.

Task 6

This is an activity for you to do next time you are connected to the internet.

Task 7

E-mail is considered to be the electronic equivalent of a letter. So if the correspondence is the type that would be kept if it were in paper form (for example an e-mail making an offer or communicating acceptance of an offer) then yes, the e-mail should be kept for a certain time (usually six years), under contract law and consumer law.

CHAPTER 2

Task 1

This is a hands-on activity. You need to start either with a new installation of Sage, or a blank company.

Task 2

This is a hands-on activity. The Name should be Publicity material, the Type is Overheads, the Category is Printing and Stationery. Sage will suggest a Ref (account number) such as 7504 or 7506, and you should accept this. There is no opening balance to enter.

Task 3

Vimal could easily forget to give the account a proper name next time he uses the package and in future he may not have any idea what sort of expense should be recorded in that account. Nobody else who uses the system will have a clue either. The moral of the story is don't use abbreviations that others might not understand, and take care with spelling too. A bit of care will save time in the long run.

Task 4

It is possible for a customer and a supplier to have the same code, because it is quite possible that a business will both sell and buy goods from the same person. Although the accounts would use the same code, the accounts would be held in different ledgers.

Task 5

This is a hands-on activity. One way to complete the task is to use the new supplier wizard and fill in as much detail as possible. When you have finished open your record (make sure that terms are agreed, if necessary) and check the details on screen against those given. The illustration in the Task shows the code MCALISTA – a better code in this situation (consistent with the alpha numeric format recommended earlier in the chapter), would have been MCALI001.

Task 6

This is a hands-on activity.

Task 7

This is a hands-on activity. Make sure that your journal has an appropriate reference and that each line has a description (use the F6 key for the second two lines). You can check your journal by clicking the Financials button, or by looking at the Activity tab of the nominal ledger accounts affected, if you wish.

Task 8

This is a hands-on activity. An example file name would be SFE_A08.XYZ, where A08 stands for Activity 8 and XYZ are your initials, but be sure to ask your lecturer or manager about the file name you should use. If you save the backup to a memory stick, keep it safe and put a label on it. It is evidence of your competence!

Task 9

This is a hands-on activity. Use the F6 key when entering the second line of the invoice, to save typing. The total VAT is £5.74 (£4.07 on the first item, which was given **net**, and £1.67 on the second, where we told you the **gross** amount). Don't forget that you can use the F9 button to calculate the net amount.

Task 10

This is a hands-on activity.

Task 11

This is a hands-on activity. You may have decided to post the different types of sales (one was products, one was a service) to different sales accounts. Remember you can rename the sales accounts to suit your particular business.

Task 12

This is a hands-on activity. Check your Final balance to the one shown at the activity.

CHAPTER 3

Task 1

This is a hands-on activity. Be sure to use the Bank … Supplier option, not Bank … Payment.

Task 2

This is a hands-on activity. Be sure to use the Bank … Customer option, not Bank … Receipt.

Tasks 3 to 12

These tasks are all hands-on activities.

Tes 7

You have the following rights:

- The right to be informed of all the information held about you by the organisation

- The right to prevent them from processing their data about you for the purposes of direct marketing

- The right to compensation if you can show that you have been caused damage by any contravention of the Data Protection Act

- The right to have any inaccurate data about you removed or corrected.

Test 8

This is false. Copyright covers the way words or notes or visual images are arranged, not the idea they convey; it protects the form or expression of an idea, not the idea itself.

Test 9

No, it is illegal to install the software on any computer unless you have purchased a licence. In fact, the latest version of Microsoft Office will not work unless you register it with Microsoft, and if you attempt to register a copy that has already been registered by someone else you will be found out. Either you or your organisation may be prosecuted.

Test 10

It should be retained for six years, because this is set down in legislation.

Test 11

The regulations cover matters such as the height of your chair and your desk, the way you arrange documents on the desk, the way you key things in and use the mouse, how you set up the software, and the importance of breaks.

Test 12

Encryption involves using a 'key' to mix-up data so that it becomes unintelligible. A key has to be supplied to 'un-jumble' the data to make it readable again. This technology is important when data is being transmitted over communications links where there is a risk of interception.

CHAPTER 2

Test 1

A field is a box on screen in which you enter data or select from a list (similar to a spreadsheet cell).

Test 2

A default is the entry that the accounting package knows will normally be made in a particular field, for example today's date or the nominal code that a purchase from a certain supplier would normally be posted to.

Test 3

Accounting codes are unambiguous and precise, they can be shorter to enter than the account name and they can determine the class of transaction eg 1000 – 1999 = income, 2000 – 2999 = expenses and so on.

Test 4

It is probably not essential to save your work because all your entries are saved as you go along. It is essential to back-up your work, however, because the program may become damaged or you may make incorrect entries next time you use it.

Test 5

When a back-up is restored all the data currently held in the program is overwritten with the data from the back-up.

Test 6

It will not be possible to change the financial year once any data has been posted to the program. At the year-end it is necessary to go through a special procedure in order to move into the next financial year.

Test 7

Details such as company name and address will appear on any documents generated by the program, such as invoices and statements, and these will be sent to customers, so you will look very foolish if you can't even spell your own organisation's details properly.

Test 8

The chart of accounts is a kind of template setting out the structure of the nominal ledger – which accounts are classed as non-current (fixed) assets, which are current assets, which are current liabilities, which are expenses in the income statement (profit and loss account), and so on.

Test 9

Sales, Purchase, Direct Expenses, Overheads.

Test 10

You must set up an account for the supplier in the purchase ledger before you can post an invoice received from the supplier.

Test 11

You can either set a default nominal ledger account when you set up the supplier account, or you can choose the nominal ledger account at the time that you post the invoice.

Test 12

This is false. The system will not allow you to post a journal that does not balance.

Test 13

Obviously, it is good practice to use the correct date for transactions in any system, but in an accounting package dates govern matters such as receivable (debtor) ageing, monthly reports, and, in particular, the way the VAT liability is calculated.

Test 14

It is usually better to post the invoice lines individually. It is essential to do so if the individual expenses need to be posted to different nominal ledger codes.

CHAPTER 3

Test 1

This is false. Receipts from customers with accounts need to be allocated to outstanding invoices. From the **Bank** menu, these receipts are processed using the **Customer** button.

Test 2

False. Errors can be corrected using the error correction facility.

Test 3

False. That would be dangerous as fraudulent, untraceable changes could be made under the guise of error correction. A memorandum of the original entry is always recorded.

Test 4

So that the monthly results can be compared with budget.

Test 5

False. The transfer should be processed by selecting **Bank** and then **Record Transfer** from the task list.

Test 6

False. Modern software and hardware are reliable but they do go wrong (as I'm sure you know). Taking a backup in Sage is quick and simple – one day it will save you!

BPP PRACTICE ASSESSMENT 1

✍ You are now ready to attempt BPP practice assessment 1. This is a modified AAT simulation, issued under previous AAT standards. This tests skills relevant to the new Learning Outcomes and to your assessment.

✍ Part 1 requires you to complete a number of hands-on tasks using a computerised accounting software package.

✍ Part 2 requires you to provide advice covering a number of issues relevant to the assessment criteria for this Unit.

✍ Answers are provided at the end of the assessment.

INSTRUCTIONS

You are advised to read the whole of this assessment before commencing in order to familiarise yourself with all of the tasks you will be asked to complete.

Check your work carefully before handing it in.

Situation

SFE Merchandising is a new business that has been set up by Charlize Veron, one of Southfield Electrical's former marketing staff. Charlize is an expert on store layout and management of inventories and she intends to sell her skills and knowledge, on a consultancy basis, to medium and large retailers to help them to optimise their sales.

Charlize has started her new venture as a sole trader and has taken on some of the risk herself. However, SFE Merchandising is part-financed by Southfield Electrical, and may well be acquired by them if this new venture is a success.

Initial enquiries have been so promising that Charlize has already voluntarily registered for VAT and intends to run the standard VAT accounting scheme, not VAT cash accounting. Some sales will be one-off sales made for cash to clients who do not need to have a credit account: any such sales will be treated as petty cash receipts.

You may assume that all the documents have been checked and authorised.

Charlize rents an office from Habgood Properties, who do not have a subsidiary (purchases) ledger account.

The business commenced trading in January 2012. Charlize has decided to use a computerised accounting package and has asked you to help with this. (The cost of the package itself should be posted to an income statement account, since it will be upgraded every year).

Financial year: January 2012

Task 1.3

Write the appropriate code numbers on the journal slip J001 below. If you think you need to set up any new general (nominal) ledger accounts then do so now. Then enter the opening balances for the business into the accounting package.

JOURNAL SLIP J001		DATE:	01/01/2012	
To post opening balances as at the start of business				
Details	Code	Debit	Credit	
Loan from Southfield Electrical			2500.00	
Capital			8238.30	
Ford Ka		4999.00		
Car tax		155.00		
Motor insurance		834.30		
Second-hand desk, chair, etc		750.00		
Bank deposit		4000.00		

Task 1.4

Tasks 1.4, 1.5, 1.6, 1.7, 1.8 and 1.9 refer to the invoices and credit notes shown on the pages that follow this page.

A number of invoices and credit notes are shown on the pages following this one. In the spaces provided on each document make a note of the customer or supplier code that you intend to use and the general ledger codes (it may pay to read Tasks 1.5, 1.6, 1.7 and 1.8 below first as they are related to Task 1.4).

Task 1.5

Identify the general ledger accounts needed, creating new ones only if necessary.

Task 1.6

Set up accounts for each of the suppliers.

Task 1.7

Enter each supplier invoice and credit note.

Task 1.8

Set up accounts for each of the customers.

Task 1.9

Enter each customer invoice and credit note.

INVOICE

Dan Industrials
Park Rise
Fenbridge
DR2 7AD
Tel 03033 952060
Fax 03033 514287

VAT Reg 520 6298 62

To: SFE Merchandising
14a, Habgood House
Dagenham Avenue
Benham
DR6 8LV

Invoice number S346219
Date/tax point 3 Jan 2012
Order number
Account number

Quantity	Description	Stock code	Unit amount £	Total £
3	Flatpack office shelving units	SH249	21.99	65.97

Net total	65.97
VAT	13.19
Invoice total	79.16

Subsidiary ledger code ....

Main ledger code(s) ....

CREDIT NOTE

Rhymand Stationery Store
7 Market Street
Benham
DR6 2PL
Tel 03033 826374
Fax 03033 826375

VAT Reg 765 9257 72

Your contact is: Bill Smith

To:
SFE Merchandising
14a, Habgood House
Dagenham Avenue
Benham
DR6 8LV

Invoice number CN0214
Date/tax point 15 Jan 2012
Order number
Account number

Description	Stock code	Unit amount £	Total £
Misprinted business cards x 150		39.00	39.00

Net total	39.00
VAT	7.80
Total credit	46.80

Subsidiary ledger code   ....
Main ledger code(s)   ....

Softwac

INVOICE

Hot House
25 Parma Crescent
London SW11 1LT
Tel 020 7652 2221
Fax 020 7652 6508

Website: www.softwac.co.uk
Email: sales@softwac.co.uk

VAT Reg 760 9259 10

To:
SFE Merchandising
14a, Habgood House
Dagenham Avenue
Benham
DR6 8LV

Invoice number	10863
Date/tax point	20-01-12
Order number	
Account number	SFEMER01

Qty	Description Stock code	Unit amount £	Total £
1	Desktop PC to your spec	1224.80	1224.80
1	Sage Instant Accounts	98.91	98.91

Net total	1323.71
VAT	264.74
Invoice total	1588.45

Subsidiary ledger code   ....

Main ledger code(s)   ....

118

INVOICE

SFE Merchandising
14a, Habgood House
Dagenham Avenue
Benham DR6 8LV
Tel 03033 542697 Fax
03033 542697

VAT Reg 524 3764 51

To: | Q Q Stores
23 Queens Road
Winnesh
DR2 7PJ

Invoice number 10001
Date/tax point 06/01/2012

Description	Unit amount £	Total £
2 days consultancy, 5 to 6 January 2012	300.00	600.00

Net total		600.00
VAT		120.00
Invoice total		720.00

Subsidiary ledger code   ....
Main ledger code(s)   ....

INVOICE

SFE Merchandising
14a, Habgood House
Dagenham Avenue
Benham DR6 8LV
Tel 03033 542697 Fax
03033 542697

VAT Reg 524 3764 51

To: Whitehill Superstores
28, Whitehill Park
Benham
DR6 5LM

Invoice number   10002
Date/tax point   16/01/2012

Description	Unit amount £	Total £
5 days consultancy, 12 to 16 January 2012	300.00	1500.00

Net total	1500.00
VAT	300.00
Invoice total	1800.00

Subsidiary ledger code   ....

Main ledger code(s)   ....

INVOICE

SFE Merchandising
14a, Habgood House
Dagenham Avenue
Benham DR6 8LV
Tel 03033 542697 Fax
03033 542697
VAT Reg 524 3764 51

To: Polygon Stores
Grobler Street
Parrish
DR7 4TT

Invoice number 10003
Date/tax point 21/01/2012

Description	Unit amount £	Total £
3 days consultancy, 19 to 21 January 2012	300.00	900.00

Net total	900.00
VAT	180.00
Invoice total	1080.00

Subsidiary ledger code   ....

Main ledger code(s)   ....

INVOICE

SFE Merchandising
14a, Habgood House
Dagenham Avenue
Benham DR6 8LV
Tel 03033 542697 Fax
03033 542697
VAT Reg 524 3764 51

To:

Q Q Stores
23 Queens Road
Winnesh
DR2 7PJ

Invoice number   10004
Date/tax point   23/01/2012

Description	Unit amount £	Total £
1 days consultancy, 23 January 2012	300.00	300.00
	Net total	300.00
	VAT	60.00
	Invoice total	360.00

Subsidiary ledger code   ....

Main ledger code(s)   ....

INVOICE

SFE Merchandising
14a, Habgood House
Dagenham Avenue
Benham DR6 8LV
Tel 03033 542697 Fax
03033 542697

VAT Reg 524 3764 51

To: Dagwell Enterprises
Dagwell House
Hopchurch Road
Winnesh
DR2 6LT

Invoice number   10005
Date/tax point   29/01/2012

Description	Unit amount £	Total £
4 days consultancy, 26 to 29 January 2012	300.00	1200.00

Net total		1200.00
VAT		240.00
Invoice total		1440.00

Subsidiary ledger code   ....

Main ledger code(s)   ....

CREDIT NOTE

SFE Merchandising
14a, Habgood House
Dagenham Avenue
Benham DR6 8LV
Tel 03033 542697 Fax
03033 542697

VAT Reg 524 3764 51

To: Whitehill Superstores
28, Whitehill Park
Benham
DR6 5LM

Invoice number CN001
Date/tax point 19/01/2012

Description	Unit amount £	Total £
Initial consultancy fee 0.5 days, 12 January 2012	300.00	150.00
Net total		150.00
VAT		30.00
Credit total		180.00

Subsidiary ledger code ....
Main ledger code(s) ....

Task 1.10

Back-up your work using a suitable file name or one suggested by your assessor.

Task 1.11

The following items should now be entered.

- A cash receipt, shown below

CASH SALE

SFE Merchandising
14a, Habgood House
Dagenham Avenue
Benham DR6 8LV
Tel 03033 542697 Fax
03033 542697

VAT Reg 524 3764 51

To: Cash sales
(Whites Bookstores)

Invoice number 10006
Date/tax point 08/01/2012

Description	Unit amount £	Total £
2 hours consultancy, paid for in cash and paid into petty cash	37.50	75.00

Net total	75.00
VAT	15.00
Invoice total	90.00

Enter via a journal with reference 10006

- The balance on the bank deposit account is transferred to the current account.

- Three payments are made to suppliers, details follow:

Date	15 January 2012
Payee	
Dan Industrials	
£	79.16
	000001

Date	18 January 2012
Payee	
Rhymand Stationery	
£	109.20
	000002

Date	24 January 2012
Payee	
Softwac	
£	1588.45
	000003

- A standing order payment to Habgood Properties (shown below) and receipts from customers (as shown on the paying-in slips below).

Standing Order Schedule		
Day in month	*Payee*	*£*
25	Habgood Properties	200.00

Cheques etc.			Brought forward £				£50		
							£20		
							£10		
							£5		
							£2		
							£1		
							50p		
							20p		
							Silver		
			Polygon Stores	1080	00		Bronze		
							Total Cash		
							Cardnet	1080	00
							Cheques etc.		
Carried forward £			Carried forward £	1080	00	Total £	1080	00

Date   23/01/2012   500001   FOR SFE MERCHANDISING   06325143

Cheques etc.			Brought forward £				£50		
							£20		
							£10		
							£5		
							£2		
							£1		
							50p		
							20p		
							Silver		
			Whitehill Superstores	1620	00		Bronze		
							Total Cash		
							Cardnet	2370	00
			QQ Stores	750	00		Cheques etc.		
Carried forward £			Carried forward £	2370	00	Total £	2370	00

Date   27/01/2012   500002   FOR SFE MERCHANDISING   06325143

- A BACS remittance advice from a customer and a petty cash slip (both shown below). For the Petty Cash slip, the train fare was zero-rated for VAT.

DAGWELL ENTERPRISES

Dagwell House
Hopchurch Road
Winnesh
DR2 6LT

BACS remittance advice

The following amount will be remitted to the bank account of

SFE Merchandising

on

31 January 2012

in payment of the following invoice(s)

10005

Amount: £1440.00

PETTY CASH PAYMENT SLIP	**Date:** 9 January 2012	PCP001
Description		**£**
Train fare		23.45

Task 1.12

Refer to the bank statement shown below. If you think you need to set up any new general ledger accounts then do so now. Then reconcile the bank statement, entering any adjustments that you think are necessary.

	BANK STATEMENT		SFE MERCHANDISING				
			paid out		paid in		balance
date	details		£		£		£
2012	Opening balance						0 00
1 JAN	DEPOSIT				4000 00		4000 00
17 JAN		000001	79 16				3920 84
18 JAN	INSURANCE	DD	43 21				3877 63
24 JAN	SUNDRY CREDIT				1080 00		4597 63
25 JAN	STANDING ORDER		200 00				4757 63
26 JAN		000003	1588 45				3169 18
27 JAN	CHARGES JAN 2011						
	SERVICE CHARGE		6 51				3162 67
31 JAN	BACS RECEIPT				1440 00		4602 67
	TOTAL PAYMENTS/RECEIPTS		1917 33		6520 00		

Task 1.13

Print the following items:

- An audit trail
- Customer statements
- Bank reconciliation
- Sales and sales returns day books
- Purchases and purchase returns day books
- Subsidiary trade receivables listing (sales ledger)
- Subsidiary trade payables listing (purchase ledger)
- Nominal ledger activity
- Trial balance

Task 1.14

On counting the petty cash you find that the amount in the tin is £66.55. Complete the petty cash reconciliation statement shown on the next page.

Task 1.15

Referring to your print-outs from Task 1.14, complete the subsidiary ledger and control account reconciliations shown on the next page.

Task 1.16

Back-up your work using a suitable file name (or the file name suggested by your assessor).

Task 1.17

Charlize is worried that one of her customers will not pay and has asked you how to show this in the computerised accounting package. Write a short note for her in the space provided (in the box that follows the reconciliations).

PETTY CASH RECONCILIATION		
Cash in hand as per print out		
Cash in petty cash tin		
Difference		
Reconciled?	Yes ?	No ?

SALES LEDGER CONTROL ACCOUNT RECONCILIATION	
Total of outstanding sales ledger balances	
Total of sales ledger control account	
Difference	
Reconciled?	Yes ? No ?

PURCHASE LEDGER CONTROL ACCOUNT RECONCILIATION	
Total of outstanding purchase ledger balances	
Total of purchase ledger control account	
Difference	
Reconciled?	Yes ? No ?

Note for Charlize concerning customer non-payment

Task 1.18

Close down the computer, making any notes that are appropriate below.

When you have completed your work, explain how you closed down the computer system so as not to cause any damage.	

Part 2 – General questions

Charlize has a number of questions for you about using computers. These are shown below.

Task 2.1

I have installed some AntiVirus and internet security software and have been seeing some strange messages on my screen, two of which I've managed to capture by doing a 'print screen'.

For this one I just clicked on OK

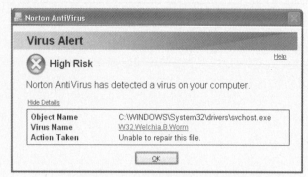

For this one I left the 'recommended' option selected and clicked on OK.

Did I do the right thing? Why do these messages appear?

Task 2.2

All of my customers are large companies. Do you think I need to register under the Data Protection Act?

Task 2.3

As you know I've agreed to share the office and the computer with another small company, and this helps to keep the cost down, but I'm a bit worried about

keeping my data safe and confidential. Do you have any advice on this? Just brief details will do.

Task 2.4

I've received the following email, and I'm very worried about this. However, when I click on the link to fill in my details I just get a message saying the page can't be displayed. What should I do about this?

-----Original Message-----
From: Barclays [mailto:users-billing2@barclays.co.uk]
Sent: 31 January
To: charlize.veron@sfemerchandising.co.uk
Subject: official Notice for all users of Barclays IBank.

Details Confirmation

SECURITY ALERT: Please read this important message

Our new security system will help you to avoid frequently fraud transactions and to keep your investments in safety.

Due to technical update we ask you to confirm your online banking membership details. Please fill the form below.

Please follow the link below to fill the form "Details Confirmation":

http://www.personal.barclays.co.uk/goto/pfsolb_login

Task 2.5

I make a full back-up every day, but this takes ages and it is like watching paint dry. Do you have any recommendations about this?

Task 2.6

Finally, am I right in thinking that once all my invoices and so on are entered into the accounting package I don't need to keep the paper copies?

Prepare your answers to these questions using word-processing software, including features such as headings, bold, bullet points and tables as appropriate.

Save your work with an appropriate file name.

Computerised Accounting BPP practice assessment 1 – answers

Tasks 1.1 and 1.2

No answer is provided for tasks that are specific to your own work environment or that involve creating back-up files.

Task 1.3

You should have entered company details for SFE Merchandising – you can find them on any sales invoice. When preparing to enter the journal you may find that you need to create a new account for Motor Insurance. Use the new nominal account wizard. We suggest the account type 'Overheads' and the category 'Motor Expenses', in which case the account number will be 7301.

Task 1.4

All purchase invoices and credit notes are posted to the Purchases Ledger Control Account (2100) and all sales invoices and credit notes to the Sales Ledger Control Account (1100).

The other codes that we would use are indicated in the following extract from an audit trail (PI = purchase invoice; PC = purchase credit note; SI = sales invoice; SC = sales credit note).

Type	Reference	Date	Subsidiary ledger	Nominal ledger
PI	S346219	03/01/2012	DANIN001	0040
PI	2149	10/01/2012	RHYMA001	7500
PI	S56729	01/01/2012	MARKE001	8200
PC	CN0214	15/01/2012	RHYMA001	7500
PI	10863	20/01/2012	SOFTW001	0030
PI	10863	20/01/2012	SOFTW001	8202
SI	10001	06/01/2012	QQSTO001	4000
SI	10002	16/01/2012	WHITE001	4000
SI	10003	21/01/2012	POLYG001	4000
SI	10004	23/01/2012	QQSTO001	4000
SI	10005	29/01/2012	DAGWE001	4000
SC	CN001	19/01/2012	WHITE001	4000

Task 1.5

You should not need to set up any new nominal accounts to post the invoices, but if you did so they should be of the correct type and category.

Tasks 1.6 and 1.8

We recommend that you use alphanumeric account codes in the subsidiary ledgers, consisting of the first five letters of the name and the digits 001, for example DANIN001.

Tasks 1.7 and 1.9

The invoice from the Market Research Society should have the tax code T2, because professional subscriptions are exempt from VAT. The invoice from Softwac should be coded to account 0030 for the computer, and account 8202 for the software.

Task 1.10

No answer is provided for tasks that are specific to your own work environment or that involve creating back-up files.

Task 1.11

Note the following points.

- The cash receipt should be posted as a journal with the invoice number (10006) as the reference: Debit Sales £75.00, Debit Sales Tax Control Account 15.00, Credit Petty Cash £90.00.

- You can use the Bank … Supplier … Pay in Full option to post the payments to suppliers. Note that the payment to Rhymand Stationery Store is made net of the credit note.

- The standing order should be posted using the Bank … Payment option. You are told in the scenario that rent is exempt from VAT, so the tax code is T2. (Note. Just in case you are wondering about this, or have different experience, it is in fact possible for a landlord to make an election to charge VAT on rent, and some landlords do this, but this is well beyond the scope of your current studies).

- Note that the second payment slip includes receipts from two separate customers, but you should give both receipts the same reference (500002). The payment from QQ Stores does not exactly match the outstanding invoices, so you should allocate the £750 to invoices in date order.

- Train fares are zero-rated for VAT so the tax code to use is T0.

Task 1.12

You may need to set up a new nominal ledger account for Bank Charges (Type – 'Overheads', Category – 'Bank Charges and Interest'). There are two items that have not yet passed through the bank account: cheque number 000002 and receipt number 500002. There are two adjustments to post, one for insurance and one for bank charges.

Task 1.13

You should arrive at the following trial balance if you enter everything correctly.

	Debit	Credit
Office Equipment	1224.80	
Furniture and Fixtures	815.97	
Motor Vehicles	4999.00	
Trade Receivables Control Account	330.00	
Bank Current Account	6863.47	
Petty Cash	66.55	
Trade Payables Control Account		99.00
Sales Tax Control Account		885.00
Purchase Tax Control Account	296.13	
Loan from Southfield Electrical		2500.00
Capital		8238.30
Sales		4425.00
Rent	200.00	
Motor Tax	155.00	
Motor Insurance	834.30	
Travel	23.45	
Office Stationery	91.00	
Bank Charges	6.51	
Subscriptions	99.00	
Insurance	43.21	
Computer Software	98.91	
TOTAL	16147.30	16147.30

Task 1.14

There is no difference between the cash in the petty cash tin and the balance of the petty cash account. Both figures are £66.55, the account reconciles.

Task 1.15

The balances of the subsidiary ledgers should equal the control account balances.

Task 1.16

No answer is provided for tasks that are specific to your own work environment or that involve creating back-up files.

Task 1.17

> **Note for Charlize concerning customer non-payment**
>
> Accounting packages such as Sage have functions to handle events such as non-payment by a customer. In Sage there is a 'Write Off, Refund and Returns' wizard, which takes the user step-by-step by through the process and posts all the necessary accounting entries.

Task 1.18

Answers will differ depending upon the specific computer environment. Your answer should cover first ensuring work is saved, then properly closing down all applications and finally following the correct procedure to shut down the PC.

Tasks 2.1 to 2.6

To: **Charlize Veron**

From: **Your Name**

Subject: **Computer issues**

Date: **31 January 2012**

Thank you for your message. I have answered your questions as best I can below, but please feel free to raise any additional queries if you need more information.

AntiVirus and internet security alerts

I am very pleased that you have chosen to install this software, and it is clearly working to protect your computer and its data.

In the case of the first message you had no option but to click on OK, but if you look carefully at the message you will note that you are told that it was not possible to repair the virus. This may be because your anti-virus software is not up-to-date or there may be another reason.

I suggest that you visit the website of the anti-virus software company and look up the virus named here (W32.Welchia.B.Worm). You are likely to find details of the virus and instructions on what, if anything, you need to do. These companies usually provide free tools for removing viruses.

You did exactly the right thing with the second message. Your internet security software includes what is known as a firewall, which prevents unauthorised persons or programs gaining access to your computer via your internet

connection. It does, however, give you the option of allowing third party access, because there may be occasions when you want to permit this.

As you say, if in doubt it is always best to choose the 'recommended' option.

Data Protection Act registration

I suggest that you look at the guidance on the relevant government website (http://www.ico.gov.uk). This will help you decide whether you need to register under the Data Protection Act.

The Data Protection Act is concerned with what is known as 'personal data', which is data about living individuals. If you ever take on employees, or if you hold data relating to people, you will need to register.

Ensure you follow the eight data protection principles. These state that data you hold about individuals must be:

- Fairly and lawfully processed
- Processed for stated, limited purposes
- Adequate, relevant and not excessive
- Accurate
- Not kept for longer than is necessary
- Processed in line with your rights
- Secure
- Not transferred to countries without adequate protection

Data security

The most obvious measures that you can take are to:

- Make sure that the office is kept locked when it is unattended
- Make sure that there are suitable fire precautions
- Stress to the person you share with the importance of behaving in a safety-conscious manner when in the office and using equipment.

I recommend that you set up user accounts on your computer. You should have at least one account for yourself and accounts for anyone else who uses the PC.

User accounts allow you to restrict what individual users can and cannot do (for instance you can stop the other user from installing any new software) and what files individual users can and cannot access.

You should set a password for your own user account(s) and make sure that all passwords are kept secret. Above all don't write them down on a Post-it note stuck to the computer!

A good password is at least eight characters long and consists of a mixture of capital letters, small letters and numbers. You should change your password at least every three months, and immediately if you suspect that someone else has discovered it.

For extra security you can also set passwords for some programs (for instance an accounting package) and for individual files. If you do that, make sure you use a different password from the one that you use to access the main system.

Email from Barclays

This is NOT an email from Barclays bank, in fact, but what is sometimes known as a hoax. This type of hoax, where the sender attempts to acquire sensitive information such as usernames and passwords by pretending to be a trustworthy organisation, is known as phishing.

You should not click on the link again, and certainly not forward the email to anyone else. The best thing to do with it is to delete it.

I suggest you look at your bank's website, which almost certainly contains further information and advice about these hoaxes. As a general rule, banks do not request sensitive information from customers by email in any circumstances.

Back-ups

It sounds as if you are making a full back-up of your entire computer system each time, so I can understand why it is taking a long time. It is unlikely that you need to back-up the entire system every day, but you should operate a daily routine of backing-up any new files that you have created and any files that you have altered during the day.

You do not say which back-up tool you are using, but it is usually possible to configure these so that (for example) they only back-up data that has changed since the last back-up, or they only back-up specific folders and sub-folders.

- I recommend that you save all files that you wish to keep safe in sub-folders within the Windows folder called My Documents. Transfer any that you may have saved elsewhere to this location.

- Then, make a separate copy of your My Documents folder and its sub-folders on removable media such as a CD-R or a flash drive ('USB stick'). Be sure to label the media in a way that makes it easy to identify and ensure it is dated. This should be stored away from the office, in case of fire or theft.

- You should then schedule your back-up software to do a daily back-up of your My Documents folder, preferably to a network location. I would be happy to help you with this if you wish. The computer can be scheduled to complete back-ups automatically, overnight.

- On a weekly or monthly basis (depending on how much new work you create each day), you should make another copy of your latest back-up on removable media such as a CD. Again, this should be properly labelled and stored away from the office, in case of fire or theft.

- Particular care should be taken with accounting data, since this is vital to the smooth-running of your business. Most accounting packages encourage you to take a back-up when you attempt to close the program down, and I recommend that you take this option whenever you have made new entries.

Finally, I recommend that you use Auto-recover facilities in any programs that offer them – this ensures that a temporary back-up is saved every few minutes while you are working on a document, and helps to guard against power failure or unexpected problems.

Document retention

Company law and tax law requires you to keep most accounting records for a period of at least six years.

It may not be necessary to keep a paper copy of accounting ledgers, so long as you have back-up files that would allow them to be recreated and printed out again if necessary, but you should certainly keep suppliers' invoices, bank statements and so on (or scanned images that could be printed) for at least the minimum period.

THE AAT PRACTICE ASSESSMENT

✍ You are now ready to attempt the AAT practice assessment for Computerised Accounting Software.

✍ This AAT practice assessment provided by the AAT uses a standard rate of VAT of 20%

✍ Section 1 asks you to input data into a computerised accounting package and produce documents and reports.

✍ Section 2 includes short answer questions.

✍ Answers are provided at the end of the assessment.

Instructions to candidates

This assessment is in **two sections**. You must prove competence in each section to be successful.

- **Section 1** asks you to input data into a computerised accounting package and produce documents and reports

- **Section 2** asks you to complete short answer questions

The time allowed to complete this Computerised accounting assessment is **3 hours**.

Additional time up to a maximum of 1 hour may be scheduled by your tutor to allow for delays due to computer issues, such as printer queues and uploading documents to LearnPlus.

It is important that you provide all documents specified in the tasks so your work can be assessed. All printed material should be **titled** and be marked with your **name** and **AAT membership number**.

If your computerised accounting system allows for the generation of PDFs, these can be generated instead of hard copy prints. Screenshots saved as image files are also acceptable.

If you are using print-outs as evidence, the only document you will be required to upload at the end of the assessment is your assessment booklet. If you have generated PDFs or screenshots instead of printing, these documents should be uploaded to LearnPlus with your assessment book. Please ensure that your training provider is aware of which option you will be using.

Computerised Accounting The AAT practice assessment – questions

Section 1

Data

This assessment is based on an existing business, Brookland Plants, an organisation that supplies ornamental plant displays and a maintenance service to local businesses. The owner of the business is Nadine Brookland who operates as a sole trader.

At the start of business Nadine operated a manual book-keeping system but has now decided that from 1 May 20XX the accounting system will become computerised. You are employed as an accounting technician.

You can assume that all documentation has been checked for accuracy and authorised by Nadine Brookland.

Sales are to be analysed in three ways:

- Plant displays.
- Plant maintenance.
- Cash sales, which arise from occasional sales of plant displays to friends.

Some general ledger accounts have already been allocated account codes. You may need to amend or create other account codes.

The business is registered for VAT. The rate of VAT charged on all goods and services sold by Brookland Plants is 20%.

All expenditure should be analysed as you feel appropriate.

Before you start the assessment you should:

- Set the system software date as **31st May of the current year**.
- Set up the company details under the name 'Brookland Plants'.
- Set the financial year to start on **1st May of the current year**.

This set-up does not form part of the assessment standards, so your training provider may assist you with this.

Task 1.1

Refer to the customer listing below:

- Set up customer records to open sales ledger accounts for each customer.
- Save your work and print a Customer activity list, which includes each customer's name, account code, credit limit and opening balance.

Customer Listing

CUSTOMER NAME, ADDRESS AND CONTACT DETAILS	CUSTOMER ACCOUNT CODE	CUSTOMER ACCOUNT DETAILS AT 1 MAY 20XX
Ennis plc 26 Highfield Road Ronchester RC17 1BG Telephone: 0161 876 4356 Contact name: Kelly Ennis	ENN01	Credit limit: £3,000 Payment terms: 30 days Opening balance: £1,698.70
Campbell Ltd 45 Green Lane Ronchester RC12 5FR Telephone: 0161 969 3221 Contact name: Matthew Jones	CAM01	Credit limit: £4,000 Payment terms: 30 days Opening balance: £2,100.00
MJ Devonish 27 Jurys Road Ronchester RC3 8HY Telephone: 0161 456 2874 Contact name: Usman Hussain	DEV01	Credit limit: £1,000 Payment terms: 30 days Opening balance: £352.50
Bell and Cooke Ltd 32 Forest Lane Ronchester RC9 7KJ Telephone: 0161 854 9327 Contact name: Jenny Holmes	BEL01	Credit limit: £3,000 Payment terms: 30 days Opening balance: £1,200.80

Task 1.2

Refer to the supplier listing below:

- Set up supplier records to open purchases ledger accounts for each supplier.

- Save your work and print a Supplier activity list, which includes each supplier's name, account code, credit limit and opening balance.

Supplier Listing

SUPPLIER NAME, ADDRESS AND CONTACT DETAILS	SUPPLIER ACCOUNT CODE	SUPPLIER ACCOUNT DETAILS AT 1 MAY 20XX
Highdown Plants Ltd 26 Growcott Street Ronchester RC4 2JT Telephone: 0161 743 0097 Contact name: Hetal Patel	HIG01	Credit limit: £4,000 Payment terms: 30 days Opening balance: £2,600.00
Lewis and Lane 45 Princes Street Ronchester RC18 7TR Telephone: 0161 834 0029 Contact name: Denise Lane	LEW01	Credit limit: £4,500 Payment terms: 30 days Opening balance: £1,800.00
Meadow Supplies 27 Jurys Road Ronchester RC3 8HY Telephone: 0161 738 2434 Contact name: John Black	MEA01	Credit limit: £2,500 Payment terms: 30 days Opening balance: £850.20
Broad Garages 32 Anderson Street Ronchester RC9 5DR Telephone: 0161 261 4486 Contact name: James Graham	BRO01	Credit limit: £1,000 Payment terms: 30 days Opening balance: £375.80

Task 1.3

Refer to the list of general ledger balances below:

- Enter the opening balances into the computer, making sure you select, amend or create appropriate general ledger account codes.

- Print a trial balance.

- Check the accuracy of the trial balance and, if necessary, correct any errors.

List of general ledger balances as at 01.05.20XX

ACCOUNT NAMES	£	£
Office Equipment	3,189.00	
Motor Vehicle	14,500.00	
Bank	4,805.80	
Petty Cash	200.00	
Sales ledger control* (see note below)	5,352.00	
Purchases ledger control* (see note below)		5,626.00
VAT on sales		1,650.60
VAT on purchases	1,276.00	
Capital		24,300.00
Drawings	4,174.00	
Sales – plant displays		6,780.00
Sales – plant maintenance		3,460.00
Cash Sales		460.40
Materials purchases	7,480.20	
Rent and rates	750.00	
Motor vehicle expenses	550.00	

* Note

As you have already entered opening balances for customers and suppliers the software package you are using may not require you to enter these balances

Task 1.4

You have received notification of a change of address and telephone number from a supplier, Meadow Supplies.

- Enter the new address and telephone number into the computer.

- Print a screen shot of the supplier's record with the new address and telephone number

The new address and telephone number are:

54 Sandy Lane
Ronchester
RC3 6RD

Telephone: 0161 456 1983

Task 1.5

Refer to the following sales invoices, sales credit note and summary of purchase invoices and enter these transactions into the computer.

Brookland Plants
46, Kirkland Street, Ronchester, RC4 0TS
VAT Registration No 476 3163 00

Telephone: 0161 743 5188
E-mail: N.Brookland@Brooklands.co.uk

S A L E S   I N V O I C E N O 080

Date: 01 May 20XX

Campbell Ltd
45 Green Lane
Ronchester
RC12 5FR

	£
Supplying plant displays for reception area	900.00
VAT @ 20%	180.00
Total for payment	1,080.00

Terms: 30 days

Brookland Plants
46, Kirkland Street, Ronchester, RC4 0TS
VAT Registration No 476 3163 00

Telephone: 0161 743 5188
E-mail: N.Brookland@Brooklands.co.uk

SALES INVOICE NO 081

Date: 15 May 20XX

Bell and Cooke Ltd
32 Forest Lane
Ronchester
RC9 7KJ

	£
Supplying new plant displays	870.00
VAT @ 20%	174.00
Total for payment	1,044.00

Terms: 30 days

Brookland Plants
46, Kirkland Street, Ronchester, RC4 0TS
VAT Registration No 476 3163 00

Telephone: 0161 743 5188
E-mail: N.Brookland@Brooklands.co.uk

SALES CREDIT NOTE NO 016

Date: 18 May 20XX

Campbell Ltd
45 Green Lane
Ronchester
RC12 5FR

	£
Return of unwanted plant display	150.00
VAT @ 20%	30.00
Total for payment	180.00

Terms: 30 days

Brookland Plants
46, Kirkland Street, Ronchester, RC4 0TS
VAT Registration No 476 3163 00

Telephone: 0161 743 5188
E-mail: N.Brookland@Brooklands.co.uk

S A L E S   I N V O I C E   N O   082

Date: 25 May 20XX

Ennis plc
26 Highfield Road
Ronchester
RC17 1BG

	£
Maintaining existing plant displays	710.00
VAT @ 20%	142.00
Total for payment	852.00

Terms: 30 days

Summary of purchase invoices

Date 20XX	Supplier Name	Invoice Number	Gross £	VAT £	Net £	Plant supplies £	Motor expenses £
02.05.XX	Lewis and Lane	X204	2,400.00	400.00	2,000.00	2,000.00	
07.05.XX	Broad Garages	M145	216.00	36.00	180.00		180.00
12.05.XX	Highdown Plants Ltd	2010	960.00	160.00	800.00	800.00	
18.05.XX	Meadow Supplies	1904	1,284.00	214.00	1,070.00	1,070.00	
	Totals		**4,860.00**	**810.00**	**4,050.00**	**3,870.00**	**180.00**

Task 1.6

Refer to the following summary of payments received from customers and made to suppliers and enter these transactions into the computer, making sure you allocate all amounts as shown in the details column.

Cheque/BACS receipts listing

Date	Receipt type	Customer	£	Details
07.05.XX	BACS	Ennis plc	1,698.70	Payment of opening balance
24.05.XX	Cheque	Campbell Ltd	900.00	Payment of invoice 80 including credit note 16

Cheques paid listing

Date	Cheque number	Supplier	£	Details
11.05.XX	002365	Lewis and Lane	1,800.00	Payment of opening balance
18.05.XX	002366	Highdown Plants Ltd	1,500.00	Payment on account
23.05.XX	002367	Broad Garages	216.00	Payment of invoice M145

Task 1.7

(a) Refer to the following receipt issued for cash sales and enter this transaction into the computer.

Receipt Number 06
Date   06 May 20XX
Received, by cheque, from Fiona Wittin for a plant display: £90.00 including VAT

(b) Refer to the following e-mail below from Nadine Brookland and enter this transaction into the computer.

E-mail
From: Nadine Brookland   **To:** Accounting Technician   **Date:** 12 May 20XX   **Subject:** Drawings
Hello   I have used the Company debit card to withdraw £180 in cash from the bank for my personal use.   Please record this transaction.   Thanks   Nadine

(c) Refer to the following cash purchases listing and enter this transaction into the computer.

Date	Payment method	Details	Amount
20 May 20XX	Debit card	Purchase of a computer printer, model number 45XK	£108.00 including VAT

Task 1.8

Refer to the following petty cash vouchers and enter the petty cash payments into the computer.

Petty Cash Voucher	
Date 08 May 20XX	**No** PC28
	£
Emergency repair to lock on office door – VAT not applicable	38.87
Receipt attached	

Petty Cash Voucher	
Date 16 May 20XX	**No** PC29
	£
Taxi fare – VAT not applicable	22.00
Receipt attached	

Petty Cash Voucher	
Date 20 May 20XX	**No** PC30
	£
Paper for printer, envelopes and pens	27.60
VAT	5.52
Total	33.12
Receipt attached	

Task 1.9

Refer to the following e-mail from Nadine Brookland:

- Make entries into the computer to write off the amount of £352.50 owing from MJ Devonish. (Ignore VAT).

- Match this transaction against the opening balance in MJ Devonish's account.

E-mail	
From:	Nadine Brookland
To:	Accounting Technician
Date:	10 May 20XX
Subject:	MJ Devonish

Hello

The above customer has ceased trading owing us £352.50. Please write this amount off as a bad debt.

Thanks

Nadine

Task 1.10

Refer to the following journal entries and enter them into the computer.

JOURNAL ENTRIES TO BE MADE 12.05.XX	£	£
Motor vehicle expenses	65.00	
Rent and rates		65.00
Being an error in the opening journal entries		

JOURNAL ENTRIES TO BE MADE 28.05.XX	£	£
Bank	30.00	
Drawings		30.00
Being an error in recording the amount withdrawn from the bank by Nadine Brookland		

Task 1.11

Refer to the following e-mail below from Nadine Brookland and enter this transaction into the computer.

E-mail
From: Nadine Brookland **To:**   Accounting Technician **Date:**   31 May 20XX **Subject:**   Petty cash
Hello Please transfer an amount of £93.99 from the bank account to the petty cash account to reimburse the petty cash float. The balance on the petty cash account should now be £200. Thanks Nadine

Task 1.12

Refer to the following bank statement:

- Enter the direct debit for rates (no VAT) and bank charges (no VAT) which have not yet been accounted for.

- Reconcile the bank statement. If the bank statement does not reconcile check your work and make the necessary corrections.

- Print the bank reconciliation statement.

<table>
<tr><td colspan="5" align="center">North Bank plc
60 High Street
Ronchester
RC1 8TF</td></tr>
<tr><td colspan="5">Brookland Plants
46 Kirkland Street
Ronchester
RC4 OTS</td></tr>
<tr><td colspan="3">Account number 00678432</td><td colspan="2" align="right">31 May 20XX</td></tr>
<tr><td colspan="5" align="center">STATEMENT OF ACCOUNT</td></tr>
<tr><td>Date
20XX</td><td>Details</td><td>Paid out
£</td><td>Paid in
£</td><td>Balance
£</td></tr>
<tr><td>01 May</td><td>Opening balance</td><td></td><td></td><td>4,805.80C</td></tr>
<tr><td>08 May</td><td>Counter credit</td><td></td><td>90.00</td><td>4,895.80C</td></tr>
<tr><td>10 May</td><td>BACS: Ennis plc</td><td></td><td>1,698.70</td><td>6,594.50C</td></tr>
<tr><td>12 May</td><td>Cash withdrawal</td><td>150.00</td><td></td><td>6,444.50C</td></tr>
<tr><td>18 May</td><td>Cheque 002265</td><td>1,800.00</td><td></td><td>4,644.50C</td></tr>
<tr><td>20 May</td><td>Debit card</td><td>108.00</td><td></td><td>4,536.50C</td></tr>
<tr><td>21 May</td><td>Cheque 002366</td><td>1,500.00</td><td></td><td>3,036.50C</td></tr>
<tr><td>24 May</td><td>Direct Debit - Ronchester
MBC - Rates</td><td>300.00</td><td></td><td>2,736.50C</td></tr>
<tr><td>30 May</td><td>Bank charges</td><td>56.00</td><td></td><td>2,680.50C</td></tr>
<tr><td>31 May</td><td>Transfer</td><td>93.99</td><td></td><td>2,586.51C</td></tr>
<tr><td></td><td>D = Debit   C = Credit</td><td></td><td></td><td></td></tr>
</table>

Task 1.13

Use the appropriate software tool to check for data errors and print a screen shot of the data verification screen. Make any necessary corrections.

Task 1.14

Print a trial balance as at 31 May 20XX. Check the accuracy of the trial balance and, if necessary, correct any errors.

Task 1.15

Back up your work to a suitable storage media and print a screen shot of the back up screen showing the location of back up data. Your assessor will tell you what storage media you should use.

Task 1.16

Print the following reports.

- The sales day book (customer invoices)
- The sales returns day book (customer credits)
- The purchases day book (supplier invoices)
- All sales ledger accounts (customer accounts), showing all transactions within each account
- All purchases ledger accounts (supplier accounts), showing all transactions within each account
- All active nominal ledger accounts, showing all transactions within each account

Please note the accounting package you are using may not use exactly the same report names as those shown above, so some alternative names are shown in brackets.

Task 1.17

(a)   Generate an aged trade receivables analysis and print a copy.

(b)   Export the aged trade receivables analysis to a spreadsheet and print a copy. You do not need to make any alterations to the spreadsheet.

Task 1.18

Print an overdue account letter for Campbell Ltd.

Task 1.19

Use the relevant software tool to clear month end turnover totals and print a screen shot of the on screen instruction to clear month end turnover totals.

Section 2

Task 2.1

In a computerised accounting system the following data entry error message may sometimes appear.

- Show the most appropriate response to this message by selecting **one** of the options in the table below.

WARNING
Date entered is outside your current financial year. Are you sure you want to continue? Yes   No

Task 2.1	✔
Select the **Yes** button, continue to enter data and take no further action.	
Select the **No** button, check the accuracy of the date entered and if necessary change it before proceeding.	
Select the **Yes** button, continue to enter data and correct any errors later.	
Select the **No** button, change the date to the current financial year and then continue to enter the data.	

Task 2.2

Several purchases invoices have been input into a computerised accounting system.

- Which computer generated report would you use to review these transactions and identify any errors?

Task 2.2	✔
Trial balance	
Aged trade payables report	
Purchases day book	
Suppliers statements	

Task 2.3

It has been discovered that the rate of VAT on one of the purchases invoices in **Section 1** was incorrectly entered at 20% instead of zero.

- Show which **one** of the following sentences is correct.

Task 2.3	✔
In a computerised accounting system it is possible to use the software corrections tool to edit the error and change the rate of VAT.	
In a computerised accounting system it is **not** possible to use the software corrections tool to edit the error and change the rate of VAT.	

Task 2.4

Accounting information is entered into the computer from different source documents.

- Which source document is used to enter a regular monthly automated payment to a supplier?

Task 2.4	✔
Bank reconciliation statement	
Cheques received listing	
Remittance advice note	

Direct debit / Standing order schedule	

In a computerised accounting system every credit customer is allocated an account code.

- Show whether the following statement is True or False.

Two different customers **cannot** have the same account code because the computerised accounting system uses the account code to identify the customer.

Task 2.4 continued	✔
True	
False	

Task 2.5

Data stored on a computer is at risk from various sources.

- Insert the appropriate risk number in the table below to match each risk to one of the situations described. You should identify the most appropriate risk for each situation and use each risk **once** only.

Risk number	Risk to data
1	Data may become corrupted
2	Data may be difficult to locate
3	Data may be lost
4	Data may be seen by unauthorised users

Situation	Risk number
There is no organisational policy for the use of passwords	
In accordance with organisational policy back-up copies of data are taken every 2 months	
In accordance with organisational policy back-up copies of data are stored on a bookshelf in a locked office	
There is no organisational policy for the naming of files on the computer	

A computer virus is a risk to data.

- Show whether the following statements about computer viruses are **True or False.**

	True ✔	False ✔
A computer virus is a piece of software that infects programs and data		
A computer virus **cannot** enter the system as an attachment to an email		

On 26 July 20XX an overdue accounts letter was sent to Jones Brothers, 27 The Parade, Wormley, WM7 4RD. You have now been asked to password protect the letter in accordance with best practice.

- Which **one** of the passwords in the table below is the most appropriate?

Password	Most appropriate ✔
Jonesletter	
WM74RD	
JB*let2607	
27Parade	

- When should a password be changed?

	✔
Once every twelve months	
On a regular basis	
If it is known to an authorised user	
If it has been used on two occasions by one user	

Task 2.6

Match the accounting data shown in the table below, to the person or persons who require that data by placing a tick in the appropriate column. You should tick each column **once** only.

Accounting data	Sales Director ✔	Credit controller ✔	Customers ✔	Suppliers ✔
Aged trade receivables analysis				
Statement of account				
Monthly sales figures				
Remittance advice				

Task 2.7

Many computerised accounting software packages allow data to be imported from or exported to other packages.

- Show whether the following statements are True or False.

	True ✔	False ✔
Data cannot be imported into a computerised accounting package from a spreadsheet package		
Data can be exported from a computerised accounting package to a word processing package		

Computerised Accounting The AAT practice assessment – answers

Section 1

Task 1.1

A table of answers is given below although this does not represent the format of answers, which will differ according to the computerised accounting package used.

Customer	A/c code	Credit limit £	Opening balance £
Bell and Cooke Ltd	BEL01	3,000	1,200.80
Campbell Ltd	CAM01	4,000	2,100.00
MJ Devonish	DEV01	1,000	352.50
Ennis plc	ENN01	3,000	1,698.70

Task 1.2

A table of answers is given below although this does not represent the format of answers, which will differ according to the computerised accounting package used.

Supplier	A/c code	Credit limit £	Opening balance £
Broad Garages	BRO01	1,000	375.80
Highdown Plants	HIG01	4,000	2,600.00
Lewis and Lane	LEW01	4,500	1,800.00
Meadow Supplies	MEA01	2,500	850.20

Task 1.3

Trial balance as at 01.05.20XX

ACCOUNT NAMES	£	£
Office Equipment	3,189.00	
Motor Vehicle	14,500.00	
Sales ledger control	5,352.00	
Bank	4,805.80	
Petty Cash	200.00	
Purchases ledger control		5,626.00
VAT on sales		1,650.60
VAT on purchases	1,276.00	
Capital		24,300.00
Drawings	4,174.00	
Sales – plant displays		6,780.00
Sales – plant maintenance		3,460.00
Cash Sales		460.40
Materials purchases	7,480.20	
Rent and rates	750.00	
Motor vehicle expenses	550.00	
TOTALS	**42,277.00**	**42,277.00**

Task 1.4

The new address and telephone number are:

54 Sandy Lane
Ronchester
RC3 6RD

Telephone: 0161 456 1983

Task 1.5 to Task 1.11

These tasks are evidenced and marked in Task 1.16.

Task 1.12

The entries in the bank account are evidenced and marked in Task 1.16

The format of the bank reconciliation will differ according to the computerised accounting package used but the candidate should provide an accurate bank reconciliation statement, which **must** be printed.

Task 1.13

The format of the answer will differ according to the computerised accounting package used but the candidate should provide a screen shot of the data verification screen which **must** be printed.

Task 1.14

The candidate should provide the trial balance.

Task 1.15

The format of the answer will differ according to the computerised accounting package used but the candidate should provide a screen shot of a correctly completed back up screen which **must** be printed.

Task 1.16

The candidate should provide the sales day book, the sales returns day book, and the purchases day book. A table of amounts to assist with the marking of the ledger accounts is given below. These do not represent the format of answers, which will differ according to the computerised accounting package used.

Sales ledger accounts	Closing balance £	Amounts not matched £
Bell and Cooke Ltd	2,244.80	1,200.80 1,044.00
Campbell Ltd	2,100.00	2,100.00
MJ Devonish	Nil	None
Ennis plc	852.00	852.00

Purchase ledger accounts	Closing balance £	Amounts not matched £
Broad Garages	375.80	375.80
Highdown Plants	2,060.00	2,600.00 960.00 1,500.00
Lewis and Lane	2,400.00	2,400.00
Meadow Supplies	2,134.20	850.20 1,284.00

GENERAL LEDGER ACCOUNTS	Closing balance	
	Debit £	Credit £
Office Equipment	3,279.00	
Motor Vehicles	14,500.00	
Sales ledger control	5,196.80	
Bank	3,270.51	
Petty Cash	200.00	
Purchases ledger control		6,970.00
VAT on sales		2,131.80
VAT on purchases	2,109.52	
Capital		24,300.00
Drawings	4,324.00	
Sales – plant displays		8,400.00
Sales – plant maintenance		4,170.00
Cash Sales		536.40
Materials purchases	11,350.20	
Rent and rates	985.00	
Motor vehicle expenses	795.00	
Travelling	22.00	
Office stationery	27.60	
Repairs and renewals	38.87	
Bank charges	56.00	
Bad debt write off	352.50	

Task 1.17

The format of the answer will differ according to the computerised accounting package used. The candidate should provide the aged trade receivables analysis, which **must** be printed, **and** the spreadsheet, which **must** be printed.

Task 1.18

The format of the answer will differ according to the computerised accounting package used. The candidate should provide a letter to the correct customer which **must** be printed.

Task 1.19

The format of the answer will differ according to the computerised accounting package used. The candidate should provide a correct screen shot which **must** be printed.

Section 2

Task 2.1

Task 2.1	✔
Select the **Yes** button, continue to enter data and take no further action.	
Select the **No** button, check the accuracy of the date entered and if necessary change it before proceeding.	✔
Select the **Yes** button, continue to enter data and correct any errors later.	
Select the **No** button, change the date to the current financial year and then continue to enter the data.	

Task 2.2

Task 2.2	✔
Trial balance	
Aged trade payables report	
Purchases day book	✔
Suppliers statements	

Task 2.3

Task 2.3	✔
In a computerised accounting system it is possible to use the software corrections tool to edit the error and change the rate of VAT.	✔
In a computerised accounting system it is **not** possible to use the software corrections tool to edit the error and change the rate of VAT.	

Task 2.4

Task 2.4	✔
Bank reconciliation statement	
Cheques received listing	
Remittance advice note	
Direct debit / Standing order schedule	✔

Task 2.4 continued	✔
True	✔
False	

Task 2.5

Risk number	Risk to data
1	Data may become corrupted
2	Data may be difficult to locate
3	Data may be lost
4	Data may be seen by unauthorised users

Situation	Risk number
There is no organisational policy for the use of passwords	4
In accordance with organisational policy back-up copies of data are taken every 2 months	3
In accordance with organisational policy back-up copies of data are stored on a bookshelf in a locked office	1
There is no organisational policy for the naming of files on the computer	2

	True ✔	False ✔
A computer virus is a piece of software that infects programs and data	✔	
A computer virus **cannot** enter the system as an attachment to an email		✔

Password	Most appropriate ✔
Jonesletter	
WM74RD	
JB*let2607	✔
27Parade	

	✔
Once every twelve months	
On a regular basis	✔
If it is known to an authorised user	
If it has been used on two occasions by one user'	

Task 2.6

Accounting data	Sales Director ✔	Credit controller ✔	Customers ✔	Suppliers ✔
Aged trade receivables analysis		✔		
Statement of account			✔	
Monthly sales figures	✔			
Remittance advice				✔

Task 2.7

	True ✔	False ✔
Data cannot be imported into a computerised accounting package from a spreadsheet package		✔
Data can be exported from a computerised accounting package to a word processing package	✔	

INDEX

REVIEW FORM

How have you used this Workbook?
(Tick one box only)

☐ Home study

☐ On a course_____

☐ Other _____

Why did you decide to purchase this Workbook?
(Tick one box only)

☐ Have used BPP Workbooks in the past

☐ Recommendation by friend/colleague

☐ Recommendation by a college lecturer

☐ Saw advertising

☐ Other _____

During the past six months do you recall seeing/receiving either of the following?
(Tick as many boxes as are relevant)

☐ Our advertisement in Accounting Technician

☐ Our Publishing Catalogue

Which (if any) aspects of our advertising do you think are useful?
(Tick as many boxes as are relevant)

☐ Prices and publication dates of new editions

☐ Information on Workbook content

☐ Details of our free online offering

☐ None of the above

Your ratings, comments and suggestions would be appreciated on the following areas of this Workbook.

	Very useful	Useful	Not useful
Introductory section	☐	☐	☐
Quality of explanations	☐	☐	☐
How it works	☐	☐	☐
Chapter tasks	☐	☐	☐
Chapter Overviews	☐	☐	☐
Test your learning	☐	☐	☐
Index	☐	☐	☐

	Excellent	Good	Adequate	Poor
Overall opinion of this Workbook	☐	☐	☐	☐

Do you intend to continue using BPP Products? ☐ Yes ☐ No

Please note any further comments and suggestions/errors on the reverse of this page or e-mail them to: paulsutcliffe@bpp.com

Please return to: Paul Sutcliffe, AAT Senior Publishing Manager, BPP Learning Media Ltd, FREEPOST, London, W12 8BR.

REVIEW FORM (continued)

TELL US WHAT YOU THINK

Please note any further comments and suggestions/errors below.

Notes

Notes